How to Buy
a Business

How to Buy a Business

Andrew St George

CHRISTIE & CO

SURVEYORS, VALUERS & AGENTS

Published by Christie & Co
50 Victoria Street, London SW1H 0NW

First published 2002

© Christie & Co 2002
http://www.christie.com

A CIP catalogue record for this book is available from
the British Library

ISBN 0-9509560-1-5

Design by Tim McPhee
Design and production in association with
Book Production Consultants plc,
25–27 High Street, Chesterton, Cambridge CB4 1ND, UK
http://www.bpccam.co.uk

Printed and bound in the UK by Burlington Press,
Foxton, Cambridge

Photographic acknowledgements
George Williams: pages 36–7, 70–1, 84–5, 202–3;
NCT Publishing (photographer: George Williams): pages 188–9;
Leonardo Media BV: pages 128–9; Mr and Mrs Matoo: pages
148–9; Malmaison Hotels: pages 108–9

Note: *During the process of buying a business, prospective
purchasers are advised to seek timely advice from appropriate
professionals and specialists (eg accountants, solicitors, valuers,
surveyors, business agents, business finance brokers, stocktakers,
etc.) Reading this book in no way obviates the need to seek such
advice or find out the latest information.*

*The experiences and views conveyed in this book may not be
appropriate to either a prospective purchaser's individual circumstances or a particular business, and any advice or recommendation within the book is followed at the reader's own risk. Neither
the publisher nor the author accepts any responsibility or liability
for any losses incurred in any business venture or other
investment conducted by the reader whatsoever.*

Contents

PREFACE *7*

ACKNOWLEDGEMENTS *8*

INTRODUCTION AND HOW TO USE THIS BOOK *9*

1   Finding the right property *15*
2   The next steps *37*
3   Finances and Business Plan *51*
4   Buying the business *71*
    Summary of Essentials from Chapters 1–4 *82*
5   How to buy a pub *85*
    Case Study *105*
6   How to buy a hotel or guesthouse *109*
    Case Study *125*
7   How to buy a restaurant *129*
    Case Study *145*
8   How to buy a retail business *149*
    Case Study *165*
9   How to buy a care business *169*
    Case Study *185*
10 How to buy a childcare business *189*

APPENDICES
1   Statutory regulations and duties *204*
2   Freehold, leasehold or franchise? *211*
3   Structural Survey and Valuation Report *218*
4   The legal foundation of your business *225*
5   Resources *229*

CHRISTIE & CO OFFICES *246*

Preface

Each day, negotiators around the country are asked for their advice on buying a business. As can be seen from the size of this book, the answer could be a very long one. That is why Christie & Co believes *How to Buy a Business* will be a valuable tool for the thousands of people who set out each year on the road to owning their own business. For those about to embark on this exciting journey, there are several important signposts that will help them to decide if the time is right to purchase a business.

If the economic environment is sound, purchasers should be encouraged to enter the market. At the time of publishing this book, interest rates were at a 40-year low, making borrowing cheap and affordable. Inflation was also low and likely to remain tightly under control – another positive sign of a stable economy. A strong domestic housing market also plays an important part in the buying process, enabling first time purchasers to realise more equity to invest in their new business. The next important factor is whether banks and lenders are keen to lend funds to potential buyers. If they are, the climate is positive for purchasing a business. Finally, if there are plenty of available properties to buy and no shortage of buyers eager to view them, the signs are in place that it is a good time to realise the dream of owning your own business.

We wish you good luck and success in your new business.

David Rugg, Chairman, Christie & Co, 2002

Acknowledgements

The idea and impetus for this book came from the wish of Christie & Co to meet clients' needs by providing a clear, concise and intelligent guide to buying a business. I am grateful to the Company for asking me to write this book and for giving me the opportunity to talk to its experts across a variety of relevant disciplines. I have received much help from many quarters, inside and outside Christie & Co, and this is the result of many hours of conversation and collaborative research. Many thanks to the following who have helped directly and indirectly by meeting, talking, arranging, researching, reading and editing:

David Beecham
Jason Briggs
Paula Burgess
Simon Burke
Bob Campany
Elaine Chandler
Shona Clark
Martin Connelly
John Crocker
Vicki Davey
Paul Emery
Stuart Ferguson
Derek Fitch
Emma Forster
Tim Gooding
Sue Gray

Steve Guesford
Charles Harrison-Pinder
Simon Hawkins
Jeremy Hill
Simon Hughes
Richard Hulyer
Donna Ingram
Huw James
Mary Loudon
Richard Lunn
Tim McPhee
Donald Malcolm
Nigel Messenger
Neil Morgan
Jon Patrick

Margy Peters
Maria Powell
Patrick Ryan
Mark Sheehan
James Shorthouse
Michaela Smith
Jane Tiney
Julian Troup
Clare Walker
Colin Walsh
Colin Wellstead
Ian Wilkie
Roz Williams
David Wrightson
Robert Zenker

An institutional thanks to the Institute of Directors for their research help; to Book Production Consultants for printing and designing the book; to my legal advisers; and to all the organisations and bodies which answered my questions and which are listed in Appendix 5.

Finally, many thanks to Chris Day (Managing Director, Christie & Co), David Rugg (Chairman, Christie & Co) and David Dean (Marketing Director, Christie & Co) for all their help, support, encouragement, patience, wit, expertise and energy.

Andrew St George, 2002

Introduction and how to use this book

This book aims to make buying a business simple and easy. It will take you through the whole process: deciding to go into business, asking yourself which business is right for you, assessing potential businesses, valuing businesses, financing and insuring your own business. You may be thinking of investing in a business, you may be thinking of changing completely the way you run your life, or you may be expanding or changing your existing business. You may be interested in owning a pub, but end up buying a restaurant; or have your heart set on a children's day nursery, but eventually decide to acquire a care home.

Wherever your starting point, this book aims to guide you through the entire process of buying a business from the moment you first make that momentous decision to the culmination of your dream when you are at last handed the keys to the door. As well as leading you through the process of choosing the right business, it shows you how to think strategically about your business, and how to ask intelligent questions about the sector you choose to enter.

Many of us have more varied working lives than our parents did and we can expect to change jobs several times during a period of 40 to 50 years. During that time, we will undertake training and re-training, acquiring new skills.

One of the greatest changes of all comes when you decide to start your own business. Often the right moment to set up on your own comes in mid-life, when you may have more money and fewer responsibilities, but plenty of time to start and establish a new venture. Your money may come from a number of sources: a matured investment scheme perhaps, or a pension, an inheritance, a redundancy payment or a mortgage pay-off. In mid-life, you are often more secure as a person, or as a couple, than you were when younger. If you have a family, your children may have reached the stage when they are leaving home. You probably have the maturity to deal with the real-life problems you will meet while running a pub, hotel, restaurant, retail outlet or care home, and you will be able to combine that with your own energy and drive.

Although not everyone arrives at buying their own business via the same route, there are certain stages along the way that most people pass through – slowly or quickly, according to circumstance and character. You may choose or be able to miss out some of these stages, but it is important at least to know what they are. There are four main phases in buying your own business:

1. ***Finding the right property*** – Chapter 1 takes you through looking to see what businesses are available on the market, viewing businesses, and understanding the importance of location. It gives an introduction to Structural Surveys and Valuation Reports, and to how to read and understand accounts.

2. ***The next stages*** – Chapters 2 and 3 encourage you to think about why you want to own or run a business, what skills and experience you can bring, and deciding what kind of business you want to buy. They give advice on raising the necessary finance and preparing a Business Plan, and on understanding cash flow projections and a Balance Sheet. Whatever the business you buy, you will have to consider some or all of these issues.

3. ***Buying your business*** – Chapter 4 explains how to

negotiate your price, secure the deal and insure every aspect of your new business.

4. *Specific business sectors* – these are covered in Chapters 5 to 10, which tell you about the range of property-based businesses available in the pub and wine bar, hotel and guest house, restaurant, retail, care and children's day nursery sectors. All these share many of the fundamentals covered in earlier chapters, but have particular characteristics that make them distinct from each other and from other kinds of business.

Included in this book are case studies and advice from people who have succeeded in starting out on their own or in building up their business, enabling you to benefit from their experience. There are also tips from Christie & Co's business agents on what makes a particular business work in each sector.

At the end of the book, you will find a number of useful appendices which cover the following:

- *Statutory regulations and duties* – the need for all businesses to meet legal requirements relating to staffing, health and safety, insurance, licensing and so on.
- *Freehold, leasehold or franchise.*
- *Structural Surveys and Valuation Reports.*
- *The legal foundation of your business.*
- *Resources.*

This book is not just for first-time business buyers. There is a wealth of expertise about the business sectors covered, so if you are expanding your own business, changing from one sector to another, or simply curious to gain experts' insights, then this book is also for you.

How to Buy a Business draws on the collective expertise and experience of both Christie & Co, which specialises in selling businesses through its 14 nationwide offices and 3 international offices, and Christie First (business mortgages, insurance and pensions). Since it was founded in 1935, Christie & Co has become the market leader in many of its chosen sectors. These range from pubs, hotels, guesthouses and restaurants to retail businesses, care homes and leisure businesses. During this time, the company has built up a comprehensive and unequalled knowledge of its markets through its records, statistics, historical data and current market knowledge. Its unrivalled network of offices throughout Britain enables its staff to combine their local expertise with knowledge of national and international trends.

The staff who work for Christie & Co – the surveyors, valuers, negotiators, administrators and managers across the UK and Europe – have pooled their knowledge and expertise about the businesses they sell. They have given me the invaluable insights and guidance which I am now able to pass on to you in this book. They have day-to-day contact with people who are selling and buying businesses. These contacts range from inexperienced first-time buyers to the largest corporate operators; from country pub owners to city hotel operators; from local children's day nursery owners to national care home operators. This range of contacts means they understand thoroughly the mechanics of how each business sector operates, and have a clear understanding of what makes a business succeed or fail. Christie & Co's staff also know how vital personal qualities can be, and recognise the importance of the energy, skills and vision that people like you bring to their chosen business.

Their colleagues in business finance brokerage have advised on where and how to raise money to buy a business, and how to structure a Business Plan and Financial Plan to support a loan application. Other colleagues have expertise in valuations, surveys, investment, stock auditing and all aspects of insurance and pensions. The combination of all this information, experience, expertise and creative business sense means that the staff of

Christie & Co and Christie First can provide timely, accurate and sound advice about buying or selling a business. I have concentrated that advice for you here in this book.

Finally, I have included a resources directory at the end of the book. It will be useful for those wanting more information about a career in the relevant sectors, about running smaller businesses and about sources of training and support.

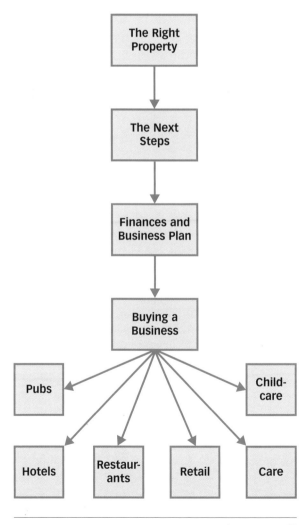

one

Finding the right property

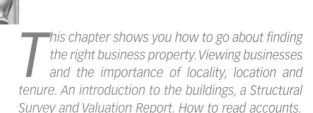

*T*his chapter shows you how to go about finding the right business property. Viewing businesses and the importance of locality, location and tenure. An introduction to the buildings, a Structural Survey and Valuation Report. How to read accounts.

Many people dream of being their own boss. Once that dream crystallises into a determination to buy your own business, you will be eager to take the first steps towards finding the ideal property to buy. It is this book's job to harness that enthusiasm and passion and take you, step by step, through the entire process. It would help you as you search for a suitable property to have had a preliminary talk with a finance broker to ascertain how much capital you are able to invest and, therefore, how much money you are likely to be able to borrow. However, most people begin by looking to see what kind of businesses are currently for sale in their chosen location and/or sector.

Finding the right business property

The more flexible you are about where you are prepared to look for a business, the more choice you will have of suitable properties and the more likely it is that you will quickly find a business you want to buy. The first thing you must do is to research your chosen region, its suitability for you and your family, and the business market. The kind of research you do will depend on the business sector you have chosen. There are many ways to find out about a market

> **"The first thing you must do is to research your chosen region, its suitability for you and your family, and the business market."**

within a particular business sector. Start with evidence that you can gather from personal contacts, from talking to owners and managers of similar businesses near you, and from information gathered from trade associations or trade exhibitions and shows. The more people you talk to, the better (see Chapter 2, pages 46–48).

Other methods of research are to use information to which the public has access and to undertake training courses and on-the-job work experience.

> "You should be able to build up a written report based on your conversations, research, Internet browsing and various enquiries."

You should be able to build up a written report based on your conversations, research, Internet browsing and various enquiries. The report – which you should put into a presentable and reproducible form – should cover the following areas:

- Your personal questions: housing, schools and amenities.
- Your business questions: competition, location and other local businesses.
- Local area information: demographics, communications and transport.

Preparation is crucial, not only because you will be thinking clearly about your new environment, but also because you will be showing your lender that you have done so. The more precise you can be, the better.

Searching for a business property is a relatively simple undertaking. You need to know where you will find properties advertised, how to go about researching the area in which the property is located, how to find out about the business competition, and how to find out about local amenities which will affect your personal life once you move. These processes are necessary, whatever business sector you choose and whatever individual business you choose to buy within that sector.

Your search should be methodical. You should

already know the kind of place you want to live in, and the kind of business you would like to run and why. You should have an idea of how much money you are going to invest and how much you need to borrow. You may well already have contacted a business finance broker. You should also have contacted a solicitor and an accountant who will work for you during the acquisition process. It helps if all these people have previous experience of your chosen market sector.

Information about businesses for sale, locally and nationally, is available from a number of sources:

- *National business agencies* – such as Christie & Co, which specialise in particular business sectors and which have national and international coverage. Put yourself on their mailing lists and join their web sites.
- *Local and regional business agencies* – these have a narrower coverage and may offer less choice of businesses. They are harder to locate, but with time and effort you will be able to identify local agencies. Make sure you are on their mailing lists.
- *Trade press* – read the trade magazines and newspapers specific to your chosen business sector in a library or on the Internet, or subscribe to them direct.
- *Local media* – make sure that you buy the local newspapers that have good coverage of your chosen area; visit their web sites.
- *Local web sites* – browse and register with local community web sites covering the village, town or region that you're interested in.
- *Word of mouth* – gossip is a good way of finding out if a business is for sale.
- *Direct* – you can always approach a business directly and say that you are interested in buying it. Alternatively, ask a business agent to conduct a search on your behalf.

If you are sent details by business agents, you will probably look at dozens before you decide to view a potential purchase. This is perfectly normal and is an important part of the process of deciding which property is most suitable for you. Make sure that you stick to the criteria of price, location and accommodation that you have set for yourself.

Viewing businesses

This, too, is a straightforward matter. Divide your attention into five areas and get as much information as you can about each:

- *The locality* – this is probably where you will be living and it is a matter of personal choice for you and your family. Think about schools, transport, amenities, culture, climate and so on.
- *The location* – this is usually of prime importance to the success of a business and dictates where your customers will predominantly come from. In addition, think about competitors, local trading conditions, average house prices in the area and so on.
- *The tenure* – this is whether the business is freehold or leasehold and is a matter, for the most part, of time and money

> *"Think about the condition of the building, any repairs needed, and any alterations required to meet trading regulations or for expansion, parking and access."*

(for more details, see Appendix 2). Think about both the long term and the short term, and how much money you can afford.
- *The building* – this is a matter of the physical state of the building which contains the business, and on which it depends; in other words, the bricks and mortar. Think about the condition of the building,

any repairs needed, and any alterations required to meet trading regulations or for expansion, parking and access.

- *The business* – this is a matter of the financial state of the business. Think about how the accounts reflect the performance of the business; compare this with other businesses of a similar size and situation.

The more information you can gather on each of these areas, the better. You can then use your fund of data about the business either to find out more by asking informed and intelligent questions of the sellers and their agent, or to check whether both are being straight with you. Remember that facts are the key here. Facts are not only those that you can check with local authorities or by simply seeing and measuring the property, but also those that are to do with reputation, competitors and, of course, your own instinct. Before you view, you should consider doing the following:

- Using the business as a customer if you can.
- Sending a friend to use the business as a customer.
- Watching the business at various times of the day to see how many customers go in or pass by. This will demonstrate not only the busiest times of the day for the business, but also the potential number of customers you could attract.
- Checking on the weekend trade at pubs, restaurants and hotels; that will help you build up a sense of the busiest and quietest periods.
- Talking subtly to competitors; ask questions but give nothing away.

On the day you decide to view, dress appropriately – think about the impression you want to create. Arrive early and drive or walk around the area to get a good feel for it. You should already have clear ideas about the location, the business sector and this individual business. Ask yourself a series of questions, all of which are important because you need to look at every aspect of the business very carefully before you commit yourself to it:

- Do you want to own this business? Why?
- What are the advantages and disadvantages of this particular business? Why?
- Would you want to be a customer of this shop/pub/ hotel/restaurant or a client of this care home/ children's day nursery? Why? What makes you decide?
- What other businesses of this type have been for sale in the last year? Have they sold or not, and why?
- Why is this business on the market? The answer may be good, bad or indifferent. The owners may be moving on to another business (but not, you hope, just down the road); they may be bankrupt; they may be cashing in before a new bypass takes trade away from the door.

> "What other businesses of this type have been for sale in the last year? Have they sold or not, and why?"

They may be retiring, sick or fed up; they may be getting out before dry rot causes the roof to fall in. Think of how complex your own life can be and think about the reasons you might have for selling this or any business. Be aware of as many reasons as you can and, when the time comes, be ready to ask the owners polite and direct questions to find out what their reasons for selling really are.
- How long have these owners been here?
- What was the business like before the current owners bought it?
- Have the present owners done all they can with the business? A busy, successful business takes energy and ideas to manage; a deserted, unsuccessful one will take as much energy and money to change. Try to talk to the owners about their approach to the

business and about what they have tried to do over the last few years.

- What changes are you planning to make and what impact will these have on the business?
- If the business was recently sold and is back on the market again quickly, be wary; it could be a great opportunity, but you could find yourself in a difficult position sooner than you had imagined.
- What role do the owners have? This is a vital question because a charismatic and innovative owner may be responsible for a considerable amount of a business's turnover. For example, in a pub or a newsagent, ascertain if the owners are a magnet for social life, or expected to be the key figures in many societies, events and celebrations. Are the owners or their family always working in the business, thus cutting staff costs and adding a strong element of personal service?

> **"What role do the owners have? This is a vital question because a charismatic and innovative owner may be responsible for a considerable amount of a business's turnover."**

- Is there a manager who is central to the business, whose departure might damage it?
- In care businesses, is the manager – who must be professionally qualified – a key figure in the business? If they left would you have difficulty filling the post?
- In pubs and hotels with a bar, is the landlord simply a manager who employs transient bar staff? Sometimes, the bar is a sort of stage and the barman is an actor; sometimes a bar is more like a confessional, and the barman is much more like a therapist or priest; sometimes the bar is the centre of a flurry of social arrangements, and the barman is essentially a secretary taking messages and providing a meeting point.
- In retail, do the outgoing owners have special

relations with suppliers and customers? Does the business depend on the character of the present owners?

- What skills do the current owners have? Do you have the same range of transferable skills? What skills would you need to acquire to be *like* the present owner? What skills could you buy in?
- Are there any reviews of the business in trade or local guides, the local media or tourist reports?

The locality and the location

Almost all the businesses covered in this book either depend upon or are sensitive to their location. Choosing where you want to buy and run a business is based on a combination of personal, local, regional, national and, of course, commercial factors.

Personal factors tend to relate to the *locality* in which a business is situated, while commercial factors relate to the *location* of the business – its social and physical environment. In the initial stages of your thinking, keep an open mind about where you want to be. The wider your search, the

> *"Choosing where you want to buy and run a business is based on a combination of personal, local, regional, national and, of course, commercial factors."*

more choice you will have; this does not mean that if you want a rural pub, you should look in city locations, but it does mean that you should consider the many opportunities available in different parts of the UK.

Locality

You should have a sense of the locality in which the business is situated. You can see when you come to view the business whether it is rural, suburban or urban; whether the area is a rich or poor one; what kind of housing is most typical and how well maintained it is; and whether there are offices, other businesses and factories nearby which might generate custom for you. You may have regional prejudices, likes, dislikes and experience. Ask around as widely as possible to make sure your sense of the area is accurate and fair.

The locality you wish to move to will be determined by many factors, such as:

- Are you able and prepared to move?
- What family commitments do you have?
- Will one or more of you have another job outside the business?
- Where will your children go to school?
- Are you culturally and spiritually suited to living in a country town or large city?
- What impact does the location of the business have on the business itself and what impact will it have on your personal and social life?

Location

The location of any business, which depends on customers coming through the door, is also determined by many factors and, in turn, dictates aspects of the business: social, demographic, physical and so on. So much depends upon the location of the business: its present level of trade, its prospects and the scope you may have for changing it. Clearly, a good location for one type of business is not necessarily a good location for another type of business, but all businesses are defined to a great degree by their location.

> *"Clearly, a good location for one type of business is not necessarily a good location for another type of business..."*

- Will your customers come to you, or will you depend on them passing by?
- Is there local transport to bring your customers to you or to visit your residents?

- Do you need a car park?
- Can you be found easily?
- Where are your competitors?
- Does the number of customers vary from day to day, throughout the day, or month by month?
- Is one side of the street busier than the other?
- What are the neighbouring businesses like?
- Is the business in a row of complementary businesses?
- What are the location issues specific to this type of business? (See Chapters 5 to 10.)

The obvious commercial qualities of the neighbourhood of your proposed business need to be set in the larger context of the national location you are thinking about. Business is subtly different in the way it is carried out all over the UK. The West Country is culturally different from the north west, which, in turn, differs sharply from Scotland, Wales and eastern England. As devolution and regional government progress, it is safe to assume that some regional differences will become more marked, even though the commercial trend towards standardised products and services delivered from central locations will continue.

Remember, while the physical aspects of a building may be changed and while the freehold or leasehold may be altered (with the landlord's consent and co-operation), its location cannot. Location is therefore important to you; if you choose a business in a poor location, or if your business does not thrive as you had hoped it would, you can, of course, attribute the performance of the business to the location. But remember, it was you who chose the location in the first place.

The tenure

All businesses occupy a building either by owning the freehold or under some form of lease. This is known as the *tenure* of the building. You should be clear about what kind of tenure you are undertaking before you start to think about the business you will operate from the building. Although the tenure of the building may be changed, it does take time and does involve some cost. The freehold of a property is the outright ownership of it – that means it is yours to sell, let, alter or demolish (depending, of course, on planning restrictions and other regulations). A lease, on the other hand, gives you the use of the property for an agreed term during which you pay rent. Further information about freeholds and leaseholds can be found in Appendix 2.

The buildings

Assessing and valuing a business is a fascinating and specialist task. There are few proprietors who fully understand the value of their own business, including its assets, the skills of its employees, its client base, its brand and its reputation. For some businesses that operate from a property – perhaps an office, factory or industrial unit – that property may be a part of the assets, but not the largest. On the other hand, for hotels, pubs, restaurants, retail outlets, care homes and children's day nurseries the property is a key element of the business and its value.

> "The property component is especially important in relation to small businesses whose owners plan to live in the same building."

The property component is especially important in relation to small businesses whose owners plan to live in the same building. The value of that building is then a principal part of the value of the business as well as the owner's home.

The main tools for valuing a business are really quite simple: a survey of the physical assets of a business (the buildings and the land), called a *Structural Survey*, and a financial and business analysis – a *Valuation Report*.[1] (See page 35.) To understand any property-based business, both a professional Structural Survey and a Valuation Report of the business property are needed. Where the owner's accommodation is in the same building as the business, as is often the case in pubs and hotels, it is important to have some sense of the basic strengths and weaknesses of the building itself – as it is for a domestic house. The complex nature of surveys and valuations of business properties means that the two are usually covered in separate documents, unlike houses. The fact is that many businesses are bought and sold without a Structural Survey, and the key document in assessing the value of the business is often the Valuation Report. The components of each are explained in Appendix 3 (pages 218–24).

How to read accounts

Many factors act together to determine the value of a business: its location, its buildings and their condition, its tenure; its assets and liabilities, its fixtures and fittings, and its

> **"The single most important factor in the value of a business as a going concern is its financial information."**

goodwill. But the single most important factor in the value of a business as a going concern is its financial information. This comprises the business's accounts, which take three forms: *Profit and Loss Accounts* (see pages 30–34), *Balance Sheet* (see Chapter 3, pages 65–66) and *Cash Flow Account* (see pages 34–35).

When you are on the point of buying or selling a business, these accounts are vitally important. Although you may be planning to *buy* a business, you must place yourself in the position of the seller. As a buyer, the accounts may be all that you have in front of you to diagnose the health of the business. As a seller, the accounts may be all that you can produce to testify to the viability of your business. It is clear that there may be times when a seller might want to emphasise profits, for example when they are just about to market the business; and there may be times when they want to emphasise its expenses or over-heads.

To be able to read the accounts of the businesses you are thinking about buying, you need to understand some basic principles of accounting. In other words, you need to know how you would express the same *incomings* and *outgoings* if they were your own. Imagine you were to represent this particular business on paper. To keep good accounts in any business you must be able to produce evidence that what the accounts suggest has actually happened. This means keeping the following, as appropriate, from the first day you do business:

- Chequebook stubs.
- Credit card receipts.
- Paying-in books.
- Bank statements.
- Receipts and invoices.
- Suppliers' invoices and receipts.
- Details of small cash purchases.
- Utilities bills.
- Rates and rents bills.
- VAT returns.
- Records of loans to and from the company.
- Salaries/wages, national insurance, tax, pensions and bonuses records.
- Income tax and other tax records.
- Professional fees.
- Stocktaking reports (where appropriate).

A cash business – retail and some licensed trades – often needs only a cash book to record income and payments made by cheque or in cash. When you come to deal with suppliers, you need a purchase book to record the goods and services you buy. If you sell goods and services by sending out invoices, you need a sales book to record the invoices as they are sent out. It is worth dividing your sales by customer so that you can monitor the volume of business from a particular client and how quickly they pay you. The sales book will indicate who is spending most with you and when, and will allow you to be intelligent about marketing further goods and services to particular customers.

Finally, you need a spreadsheet or a ledger book, which records all of these categories in the same place. This is the legacy of what is known as double-entry bookkeeping: the keeping of a general ledger which is the basis of the main accounting system used in Western business since the 15th Century. The principle is simple; however, the practice can be somewhat more complex. The general ledger records every debit and credit of the business. The general ledger is doubly linked to your sales book and to your purchase book. In it, you have a sales account and a payments account, and all your customers and suppliers have corresponding accounts. Information is therefore entered doubly. Every sale you make is a debit in your customer's account in the sales book and also a credit to you in the sales column of the general ledger. Every payment you make is a credit to your supplier's account in the payments book and also a debit to you in the payments column of the general ledger.

> **"Be sure to have more than one copy of your records – keep a duplicate copy off the premises in case of fire."**

If you are registered for value added tax (VAT), you will need a VAT column in the sales and purchase books to help you compile your quarterly return to Customs and Excise. An accounting spreadsheet will calculate the rates of VAT or any other taxes or duties due on goods that you sell. In addition, you will need a petty cash book for those small expenses that must be settled in cash – local travel, parking, window-cleaning and so on.

Of course, an accounting spreadsheet will do much of this work for you. Be sure to have more than one copy of your records – keep a duplicate copy off the premises in case of fire. You may decide to have business software to help you keep track of the wages, tax, national insurance, pensions, bonuses and so on relating to any staff you may have, part-time or full-time.

If figures and accounting are not your strength and your time would be better spent running the business and dealing with customers, it would be well worth your while to employ a bookkeeper or an accountant to keep on top of the financial paperwork.

Reading Profit and Loss or "P & L" Accounts

Reading accounts is an art, not an exact science. If you ask to see the accounts of a business that you plan to buy, you must look at them with a sceptical and rational eye. The best you can hope for is that a professional business valuer – often someone acting for a bank or mortgage loan company – will produce what they call *reconstituted accounts*. These are accounts that have had removed from them all those factors which are peculiar and particular to the present owner. For example, they may have very high transport costs, finance costs, or extraordinary building and maintenance expenses which have little to do with the fundamental operation of the business. These are costs which, if you were the owner, you would not have to take into consideration.

> "The best way to look at accounts is to take as long a view as possible and to examine the accounts for the last few years."

The best way to look at accounts is to take as long a view as possible and to examine the accounts for the last few years. If you are buying an existing business, the seller should be able to provide you with accounts for at least the last year and ideally for the last three. If there are no accounts, be very suspicious. One of the exceptions to this is the sale of pubs by a brewer/pub company, where no accounts are available. In these instances you may be able to obtain barrelage figures which will give an indication of recent levels of trading. Looking at the accounts of a business over a number of years can be difficult – for good or bad reasons. As a result, if you are not confident about your ability to read accounts, you could save yourself from making expensive mistakes by employing an accountant to do this for you. In any event, you should always take professional advice when interpreting accounts before you make a decision to buy.

Having read the accounts, you will have a picture – but not a complete one – of the business. A set of accounts can take various forms – electronic, paper or book – and may or may not have been audited by an accountant. It would be a rare seller who insisted on selling a business without showing some sort of accounting information to the potential buyer; and it would be an unwise buyer who did not insist on seeing some.

Every business is different, and each has its own accounting methods. Likewise, every business produces data which can be re-presented as accounts. When you are running a business, accounts need to be produced frequently – usually every 30 days – not just for the annual or quarterly visit to your accountant or for the tax inspector. At the end of each month, you should know whether your business has been profitable or not, whether you have enough money to cover the immediate expenses, and whether sufficient money will be coming in to cope with next month's outgoings.

> *"It would be a rare seller who insisted on selling a business without showing some sort of accounting information to the potential buyer; and it would be an unwise buyer who did not insist on seeing some."*

Anyone who has run a successful business will have organised their financial records and data along these lines.

Monthly accounts need not be complex, but they should give you a clear idea – perhaps along with a quarterly or annual report from a professional accountant – of the health and wealth of the business. Each year, depending on how the business is set up, the owner needs to file a tax return and perhaps a company return; accounts are essential to this. Everyone has a different idea about what constitutes a business profit or a business expense, and it is worth finding an accountant who shares your views and who understands your particular requirements.

Good, dependable and accurate management accounts should show trading accounts and profit and loss for every month. There is no special or fixed way of drawing up accounts but, whatever methods are adopted and whatever items of expense are included, the accounts should be consistent. Since everyone keeps accounts slightly differently, it is worth taking some time to examine the broad categories people use to think about money in business. Here are some typical categories of business expense which would usually appear in Profit and Loss Account:

- *Cost of materials* – the cost of goods or stock used over one year.
- *Overheads (fixed)* – these include rent,[2] rates, interest on loans, insurance, professional fees (accountant, solicitor), depreciation, provision for long-term projects.
- *Overheads (variable)* – these include wages, utilities bills, marketing, telephone and travel expenses (rail fares, car costs).
- *Start-up costs* – these "one-off" expenses include building or buying premises, goodwill, plant and equipment, office fixtures and fittings, utilities transfer, buying costs (professional fees).

Alongside accounts, you should be able to look at the following for the business you are thinking of buying:

- Quarterly VAT returns.
- Stocktaker's figures and stock suppliers' receipts.
- Bank statements.

You and your accountant will have to decide whether the accounts represent the true state of affairs; this applies to the Profit and Loss Account, Balance Sheet and Cash Flow Account. Here are some reasons why they might not:

- Profits may be inflated in order to gain a sale, or deflated to avoid tax.
- Accounts may include items which will be irrelevant to you (eg different interest payments on loans, different travel costs).
- Operating costs reported in a Profit and Loss Account differ from the time the costs are incurred; for example, you pay for utilities in retrospect and insurance in advance.
- Sales figures are the value of goods supplied to customers, whether they have been paid for or not. In a pub or shop, for example, most sales are in cash and are therefore received immediately; but there may be circumstances in which the business has not yet received what it is owed.

> "Accounts may include items which will be irrelevant to you (eg different interest payments on loans, different travel costs)."

- The cost of goods is calculated without VAT at the prevailing rate. Weekly and monthly sales of goods are often represented including VAT, because that is the actual amount of money that goes into the till. Accounts should always be shown with the VAT excluded.
- Do the accounts show the turnover of the business you are interested in? Some vendors may increase

the takings of the business they are selling by including profits from another business they are running separately; for example, catering for outside functions may be included in the figures for a pub. Some may include the figures for another enterprise within the same group as the one you are considering buying. Other vendors may emphasise costs and depreciation in order to reduce the tax that they have to pay. It should be noted, however, that the Inland Revenue only accepts certain rates of depreciation for tax purposes.

Normally a valuer will calculate a figure known as the *Adjusted (or Reconstituted) Net Profit*. This is the figure your valuer thinks you should be able to make, given your specific circumstances, but before bank interest and depreciation charges have been made and your own salary/drawings have been calculated. From the accounts you should be able to tell if the business is well run, if it is over-priced for the amount of trade involved, and if there are areas of the business which you can either extend or operate better than the current owners.

Reading a Cash Flow Account

This is the most important expression of the health of a business. If a business runs out of cash, it fails. A Cash Flow Account consists of two elements:[3]

Incoming

- Payments from customers.
- Grants.
- Share purchases.
- Sale of assets.
- Bank loans.
- Tax refunds.
- Interest on investments.
- Dividends on investments.
- Sale of a business.

Outgoing

- Payments to suppliers.
- Salaries/wages.
- Acquisitions.
- Loans repaid.
- Taxes paid (including VAT).
- Interest paid.
- Dividends paid.
- Assets bought.
- Other expenses such as insurance payments.

In the licensed trades, to take one example, many of these categories will either not exist or not apply. The important items in a pub's Cash Flow Account are receipts from customers in the incomings; and payments to suppliers, wages and business expenses in the outgoings. For businesses such as pubs, what you need to focus on is the cash produced by, or consumed in, the daily running of the business. The key figure for all pub accounts is the turnover of the business: how much money is actually coming in.

> *"For businesses such as pubs, what you need to focus on is the cash produced by, or consumed in, the daily running of the business."*

Notes

1. Many larger businesses carry out regular re-valuations to enable them to make informed decisions about their properties.
2. Commercial rents are generally due quarterly: in England and Wales on 25 March, 24 June, 29 September and 25 December; in Scotland on 2 February, 15 May, 1 August and 11 November.
3. Accounting Standards Board.

two

The next steps

*T*his chapter will help you decide if going into business for yourself is the right move. How to assess yourself and your skills, and compile a CV. How to decide on the kind of business you want to buy and run. Information gathering. An introduction to the legal foundation of your business.

You now have a good idea of what is involved in finding the right business to buy. The next step before you purchase a business is to take the time to make sure that owning your own business is the right move for you, and that you are clear about what kind of business you want to buy.

Know yourself

Buying your own business is an exciting and satisfying project that should allow you to organise your working life as you want. In return for your hard work, commitment and energy, you will be in charge of your future.

You may have others to consider and include in your decision-making process: family, partners, friends, colleagues. However, as the owner and manager of your own business, ultimately the decisions are yours and yours alone.

> "Buying your own business is an exciting and satisfying project that should allow you to organise your working life as you want."

Before committing yourself to buying a business, you need to be clear about your priorities, wants, needs, hopes and plans over the next few years and the longer term. The work you do on yourself will require you to be honest, unblinking and self-critical because one of the greatest assets in your business is you. This step is not easy, but having taken it, you will emerge stronger and more self-aware.

The qualities that will help you succeed in a business are your own entrepreneurial skills: optimism, energy, self-confidence, ambition, integrity, passion about results and attention to detail. And, if luck is a quality, you will need that too. It takes more than one single talent to run a business. You should ask yourself the following questions:

- Are you self-disciplined and do you get things done?
- Do you have support from your family and/or partner?
- Can you work hard, sometimes seven days a week?
- Can you get along with people?
- Can you manage under stress?
- Do you persevere?
- Can you learn from mistakes?
- Can you take advice?
- Can you take a long view?
- Are you in good health?
- Do you have definite aims?
- Do you know the risks?

Preparing your CV

In the 2000s, we can rely on having three to six changes in career direction in our working life. To move confidently from one field to another you must be clear about the skills you have and how they might be freshly applied, enhanced or extended. The most useful exercise you can do at this stage is to write down all the skills and experience you have in the form of a *Curriculum Vitae* (CV).

> "A CV is vital... because it will show others – lenders in particular – that you have the right skills for the business you plan to buy"

A CV is vital, not only because it helps you think about yourself clearly, but because it will show others – lenders in particular – that you have the right skills for the business you plan to buy. Increasingly, banks and lenders are willing to lend to entrepreneurs of quality and energy. They are prepared to back the right kind of individual with the right idea. Presenting both yourself and your business idea in the best possible way to potential lenders is a vital part of securing the funding you will need to buy the business you want.

A good CV should be no more than two pages long. Start with your most recent employment and work back in time. List the jobs you have done and summarise the key tasks and responsibilities these entailed. Include any training courses or skills acquired and any notable achievements. On another piece of paper, make a note of any skills you feel you should acquire before buying your own business, and any skills you would need to buy in.

You should also compile a list of what professional recruiters call your *transferable skills* – those skills that derive from one area of experience and that can be applied to another. These are distinct from aspects of your character – *determined, works well under pressure, pays attention to detail, intuitive, persistent,* and so on.[1] (See page 49.) Transferable skills are those skills that have

> **"Transferable skills are those skills that have helped you – and perhaps your employer – achieve, win business, improve the workplace, increase profits and so on."**

helped you – and perhaps your employer – achieve, win business, improve the workplace, increase profits and so on. What are the skills that enable you to do those things?

You can improve and augment your skills by joining classes or taking short courses, by working for others, by talking, reading and learning. There are many training courses and a great deal of literature on starting your own business.[2]

There is no set formula for a good CV, but it should be clearly printed on white paper and include the following:[3]

- *Personal details* – names, address and contact details.
- *Education* – any recent or relevant qualifications.
- *Work, experience and skills* – any relevant details.
- *Activities and interests* – use these to give a rounder sense of yourself.
- *Referees* – people who can speak honestly for you.

What kind of business do you want to buy?

Choosing a business can be great fun. Each set of details you pore over and each business you view will help you clarify the kind of business best suited to you and your skills and experience. The clearest path is often to set up in a business that you know already. A chef working for someone else might buy their own restaurant; a hotel manager or barman might take on their own hotel or pub; a family doctor or nurse might buy a care home; and a teacher might set up a children's day nursery.

Few businesses give the scope to start small and still make a profit, as well as holding out the possibility of expanding as you learn and grow more confident. Fortunately, service industries such as retailing, hospitality and care allow you the opportunity to acquire new skills as you work and grow into your new role. In addition, none of these sectors requires specialised or advanced training of any great length, although there are legal requirements for those in the licensed trades. The care sector can provide a range of opportunities and the scope for good profits. As lifestyles, demographics and working practices change, so will the need for additional care services for both the young and the old. You need no special training to own a business of this kind, but you do need specific training to run one.

Choosing the right business for you is a critical matter. Here, we can cover in detail only businesses in the retail, licensed, leisure and care sectors. These themselves provide wide scope for all kinds of skills, and they often have the added advantage of allowing the owner to live on the premises. Many of the skills necessary to run one business can be transferred to another: financial planning, marketing, handling staff and business development are all skills that you can apply across a range of businesses.

There are three kinds of business – irrespective of their commercial activity – that fall within the scope of this book. They can be defined according to the lifestyle which naturally goes with them. They are as follows:

- Lifestyle businesses.
- Entrepreneurial or commercial businesses.
- Multiple businesses.

Ask yourself what kind of business life you want to live, ideally. Do you want to make money first and foremost? Do you want to build up the business, sell and move on? Do you want to establish a chain of similar business units? Do you want to retire in 5, 10 or 15 years and be supported by the business? Do you want the capital value of the business to grow? Do you want to take maximum profits from the business in the short term? Do you prefer to work alone, or in teams? Do you enjoy building up a business and employing people to help you? Do you like to see your ideas put into practice?

Lifestyle businesses

Many people choose businesses that allow them a more relaxed lifestyle, as opposed to making high profits. These people are concerned with their health, their environment, the pace of their life, their community and so on. They tend to buy what professional business agents call *lifestyle businesses*. These businesses allow you the freedom to do such things as:

- Organise your time.
- Work for yourself.

- Live where you want, often in a rural or village setting.
- Choose your working environment.
- Operate the business on your own without the added complication of having to employ staff.

A lifestyle business should also give you freedom *from* the following:

- Unpleasant environments.
- Unreasonable working conditions.
- Office politics.
- Nine-to-five routine.
- Long-distance commuting.

In general, those who are attracted to lifestyle businesses tend to be less interested in money and more interested in the quality of their working life. They may have other sources of income, or be less dependent – emotionally or financially – on the business. Typical lifestyle locations tend to be in rural areas unspoilt by development, and in pretty country towns and villages. If you are attracted to such a business, it is worth searching widely throughout the whole country, since you need to combine location with a sustainable business. Typical examples of lifestyle businesses are a small guesthouse, a rural retail outlet or post office, and a village pub.

> *"Do you enjoy building up a business and employing people to help you? Do you like to see your ideas put into practice?"*

Entrepreneurial or commercial businesses
Entrepreneurial or commercial businesses tend to be a much more straightforward proposition. Of course, there can be no fixed rules, but people who are attracted to these businesses are willing to trade their working environment for higher profits. Such businesses can

operate where there is a sufficient clientele for what they offer. They can be found throughout the country, usually in areas of high population density, and they bring the advantages and disadvantages of urban life.

Such businesses require a full commitment of time and energy. Running them often means employing staff, working every day of the year, or arranging for someone – a manager perhaps – to cover for you. The commitment is greater, but the financial rewards are potentially higher.

Multiple businesses

While it is fair to say that many business owners invest much of themselves along with their money, there is a category of business buyer – in reality an investor – who is interested in developing a chain of businesses. People like this usually specialise in one of the sectors covered in this book. Their aim is to build an empire and run it; they may be less interested in the business once it is running at a profit, and more interested in moving on to increase their share of the market by adding another business to their portfolio.

> *"If you invest in one or more properties... you have to be prepared to trust others to manage certain aspects of your business for you."*

If you invest in one or more properties which you plan to expand, you have to be prepared to trust others to manage certain aspects of your business for you. Since you cannot be everywhere at once, and since your business's reputation is one of its most valuable assets, you must appoint good staff and managers. You must be competent at managing others and at dealing with the larger issues of planning and strategy.

What kind of business do you want to own/run?

This book concentrates on pubs, hotels and guesthouses, restaurants, retail stores (post offices, newsagents and convenience stores), care homes and children's day nurseries. Much of what you read here will apply to all these commercial sectors; the approach to buying a pub and a care home, a restaurant or a hotel is fundamentally the same in terms of how to borrow finance, plan, search for and assess the business.

All these businesses will allow you to do the following:

- Own your business.
- Work for yourself.
- Start in business with minimal training and qualifications.
- Plan your personal and business life.
- Live where you choose.
- Live at the business (providing there is owner's accommodation).

> *"As you think about typical customers, think about whether you enjoy dealing with the type of people the business will attract..."*

While there is plenty of common ground, there are clear differences between the sectors which make them more appropriate for one person than another. This is not to say that if you become skilled at running a pub you could not or should not consider running a hotel. For example, you may start by searching for a post office or newsagents and eventually decide to run a pub instead.

One way to define and sharpen the differences between these sectors is to think about what typical customers want from you. A customer buying a newspaper is not the same as a client buying several years in a care home; a customer at a bar does not want the same kind of thing as a corporate client looking to run conferences in your hotel. As you think about typical customers, think about whether you enjoy dealing with the type of people the business will attract:

- Retail and post offices will attract a broad demographic spread.
- Pubs will attract those who enjoy drinking and eating.
- Guesthouses and smaller hotels may well attract a certain type of holidaymaker.
- Larger hotels may have a mixed clientele of business customers and tourists.
- Care homes will have a wide range of clientele but may be socially specific, according to the provision and make-up of the particular home.
- Children's day nurseries will draw a wide social mix of parents and children.

What you must do is match your skills and inclinations to the realities, the lifestyle and the customers you might reasonably expect in a particular sector.

Information gathering
Word of mouth

Talk to as many people as you can who are in both the business sector you choose and the geographical area where you plan to buy. Ask all those questions that only a business owner could answer. Be polite, and don't waste people's time. Remember that they can speak only from their own experience. As you talk to more contacts, you will be able to put together a rounded understanding of the sector that interests you. The more specific your questions the better, although you should leave space for some more general ones so that you can get a feel for the business sector and a sense of its culture and values. Examples of some of the questions you may wish to ask are:

- Why did you go into this business?
- What were you doing before this?
- What made you move?
- How did you identify your business property?

- How did you raise the necessary money?
- How did you deal with the vendors and their agent?
- Are you happy with the business as it is?
- How much money are you making?
- Has it provided the lifestyle you hoped for?
- What personal and family considerations did you take into account?
- What would you change about the business – and to what?
- What are the major mistakes you made?
- What have you learned?
- What has been your greatest success in the business? How did you achieve it?
- What is your list of "dos" and "don'ts"?
- How do you deal with customers, suppliers, regulatory bodies and so on?
- What are your plans?

In addition to business owners, talk to business agents, brokers, lenders and experts in each field to get a sense of the territory you are about to enter.

> *"There is a wealth of publicly-available information from all manner of sources, including national and local newspapers and the trade media..."*

Public information sources

There is a wealth of publicly-available information from all manner of sources, including national and local newspapers and the trade media (see Chapter 1, page 18), which will help you build up a clearer picture of the sector that interests you. For example:

- Government departments and web sites.[4]
- Business directories.[5]
- Local authorities.
- Local libraries.
- Business associations, Learning + Skills Councils, Chambers of Commerce.[6]

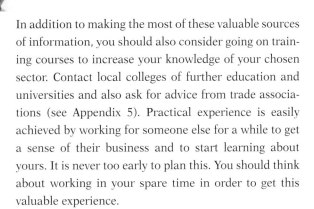

In addition to making the most of these valuable sources of information, you should also consider going on training courses to increase your knowledge of your chosen sector. Contact local colleges of further education and universities and also ask for advice from trade associations (see Appendix 5). Practical experience is easily achieved by working for someone else for a while to get a sense of their business and to start learning about yours. It is never too early to plan this. You should think about working in your spare time in order to get this valuable experience.

> *"Practical experience is easily achieved by working for someone else for a while to get a sense of their business..."*

The legal foundation of your business and how you will trade

Once you have an idea of the issues surrounding locality, location and the type of business – or at least have a sense of what information you need about yourself and about the business to address these issues properly – you must decide how you are going to trade. This means determining the legal form your business will take. The decision may depend on your circumstances or inclinations:

- Do you want to work on your own?
- Do you want to work with business partners, some or all of whom may be members of your family?
- Do you want to own and manage your business?
- Do you want to own and expand your business?
- Do you want to create a company that is financially separate from your personal assets?

As far as how you will trade is concerned, there are four options for you to choose from: *Sole Trader*, *Partnership*, *Limited Liability Partnership* and *Limited Company*. The simplest form of business is that of a Sole Trader, either in your own name or in a business name. All four options are explained in Appendix 4. Depending on which option you choose, different taxation rules will apply. You should seek professional advice before deciding which is best suited to your particular commercial and personal requirements.

Notes

1. This list is adapted from *What Color is Your Parachute: A Practical Manual for Job-Hunters and Career Changers*, by Richard E Bolles (Ten Speed Press, 2001). This book has been published yearly since 1970.

2. Sources of help: The Learning + Skills Council (formerly the Training and Enterprise Councils – TECs), Local Enterprise Companies in Scotland; the Small Business Service (formerly Business Link), Chambers of Commerce, Department of Trade and Industry (DTI); use the telephone listings under Business Enterprise Agencies. See also *Hooked on Helping Business*, DTI ref. 01/704.

3. See B Hoopson and M Scally, *Build Your Own Rainbow* (Lifeskills Associates, 1991).

4. For example, Department of Trade and Industry; Employers' Helpline (0345 143143); Companies House; Office for National Statistics; Office of Fair Trading. See Appendix 5.

5. For example, *The Retail Directory*, Newman Books (32 Vauxhall Bridge Road, London SW1V 2SS); *Thomson Directories*; *Croner's Reference Book for Self-Employed and Smaller Businesses*.

6. The Learning + Skills Council (formerly the Training and Enterprise Councils); (Local Enterprise Companies in Scotland); Small Business Service (Small Business Gateway in Scotland, Business Connect in Wales). See also *Hooked on Helping Business*, DTI ref. 01/704.

three

Finances and Business Plan

*T*his chapter shows you how to find a lender, borrow money and use a business mortgage broker. The importance of a Business Plan and financial information. How to get professional advice.

Before you decide to enter a particular business sector and identify a business you want to buy, you have to answer two financial questions. How much money are you prepared to spend on it? And, secondly, if you need to borrow, who will lend the money to you and how much?

You answer the first by fixing the price range that your financial status allows. You may think it wise to talk immediately to a reputable business mortgage broker (see pages 54–55) who will work with you to assess the maximum purchase price that is appropriate in your circumstances. There are distinct advantages in knowing your budget before you begin your search for a business. You should add in the likely costs of removal, legal and professional fees, stamp duty, stock and any immediate refurbishment costs. The initial discussion with a broker will enable you to focus on those businesses that you can afford.

> **"You must have a specific business in mind before you write your Business Plan, although there are some elements you can prepare beforehand."**

The process set out in the following pages – of talking to a broker, arranging to borrow money, and then presenting a Business Plan based on a specific business – happens neither neatly nor sequentially, but rather simultaneously and chaotically. These three stages are inter-related:

- You must have a specific business in mind before you write your Business Plan, although there are some elements you can prepare beforehand.

- You cannot compile your financial information until you have an idea of the value and purchase price of the business you plan to buy; the performance of the business itself may determine how much money you can borrow.
- All lenders will want a Valuation Report on the business you plan to buy. This will help determine how much money you can borrow.

Handling the timing of these stages can be tricky. This is why a good broker is useful, not to say essential, taking you through the process and co-ordinating the stages with you.

Borrowing money

First you must decide whether you want or need to borrow money. You may have an investment, inheritance, pension lump sum or redundancy lump sum to use which will allow you to buy a business outright. Or you may want to invest some of your assets in a business and use the business to finance the borrowing costs – if so, you should be clear about how you are going to fund this.

There are many institutions where you can get the money you may need to buy your business. Where you go will depend on how much you want to borrow and how much it costs to borrow; on the length of the loan, on the state of the business and on the record you have as a borrower. It may also be determined by the fact that some banks specialise in particular markets and, as a result, are keen to lend to aspiring purchasers in those markets. As a business buyer, you can finance your purchase by borrowing money from a lender or by selling a share in your business to a partner. The first of these is called *debt funding* and the second is called

> "A good broker is useful, not to say essential, taking you through the process and co-ordinating the stages with you."

equity funding. Debt funding is quicker to set up, keeps you in control of the business and leaves you in possession of the business when you sell. Equity funding involves a partner whom you must pay out of profits, requires you to share control of the business and means you split the proceeds from the sale of the business when you sell it. Finding an equity partner can take a long time.

You can borrow money from family, friends and banks or through general mortgage brokers, business mortgage brokers,[1] (see page 69) venture capital firms[2] and business angels.[3] You can also borrow against the accumulated value of an occupational pension (subject to the Trustees' consent, where required). While there are many advantages to this, it can be a technical and com-

> *"The broker should know about the best deals and the most competitive rates in a market. These can change from one minute to the next."*

plex matter, and you should use specialist advice. The simplest of these sources of money is, without question, a lender who understands the business and has a professional sense of what you are trying to achieve. A reputable broker will give you access to the right lender. The broker should know about the best deals and the most competitive rates in a market. These can change from one minute to the next. As financial markets can change at the speed of light, it helps to have a broker watching them for you so that you have all the information available when you borrow. A good broker will search for the best deal for you from the lenders available at any given time, and will make sure that you make the best possible case for borrowing so that your proposal finds approval and your loan application is successful. Business buyers who do not use the services of a broker are likely to be either buying with cash or continuing a business relationship with a lender they already know. Even if this applies to you, it might be worth checking that you have seen all the financial data you want before you make a commitment to a lender.

Using a good broker who has a series of close relationships with lenders also gives you free time, at the very point you need it, to manage all the other aspects of buying your business. The savings you make in time, the benefits you gain in access to the best market rates available and the advantages you derive from using a broker's network of information should cover the fees a broker will charge you. As with all professional advice that may appear costly at the outset, you should ask yourself if you are prepared to take the risk of doing without it.

How much you can borrow depends on so many personal variables that it is impossible to give general advice. There are, however, three important factors that all lenders consider:

- How much of your own capital are you putting towards the purchase price of the business?
- What skills, experience and ideas are you bringing to the business?
- What level of debt can the business itself sustain?

Of these, the first is the most important. The greater the proportion of your own money you are willing to put into the business, the more readily you will be able to borrow the rest. Secondly, lenders will look at your own records, assets and track record; you will have a chance to put your skills and experience before them, and impress them with the quality of the approach in your Business Plan. Thirdly, they will assess the security of the individual business, its value (assessed in a Valuation Report – see Appendix 3, pages 221–4) and its capacity to support a loan. Where there is no accounting information available, a lender normally limits the loan to a percentage of the freehold valuation, not to a percentage of the overall value of the business.

Apart from the amount you want to borrow, the terms of repayment and the rate of interest, one of the prime considerations when you are buying a business is the timing of your loan. Often you have to move quickly, or even to have some funding arranged before you make an offer on a business. A business mortgage broker should understand the time constraints you have, the business sector you are entering, and what might be expected or normal in your commercial position.

As part of your approach to buying your business, you should set aside time to prepare a Business Plan, compiling Financial Information, making cash flow projections and formulating a Balance Sheet (see pages 63–7).[4] Even if you have not formally written these, a good broker should take you through the steps so that it is easy for the lender to lend you the money you need; this is why you should deal with someone who knows the business sector you are buying into. Any lender will need to see the following:

> *"Often you have to move quickly, or even to have some funding arranged before you make an offer on a business."*

- *Business Plan* – summary, business idea (location, property, market and market size, competition, sales, management, expansion, risks), product or service, staffing and resources, pricing, Marketing Plan.
- *Financial Information* – including a Profit and Loss Forecast, cash flow projections, Balance Sheet.
- *Personal and professional references*.
- *Accounts from the existing business*.
- *Valuation Report and Structural Survey* (see Appendix 3).
- Details of any security you can offer for the loan (usually assets you own).

In your discussions with lenders, it helps to understand how they are thinking. Lenders must answer this question: will this business be successful? Many banks see lending to buy a business as essentially a continuation of the business; you might want to show how your improvements would enhance profitability and therefore the capacity of the business to support a loan. There are relatively stable lending ratios and loan arrangements across all the sectors – pubs, hotels, restaurants, retail outlets, care homes and children's day nurseries – which are the result of an efficient market. Lenders have a clear idea about how much they are prepared to lend you to buy a freehold or lease over a certain period. Clearly these ratios alter with interest rates; a good broker will research the offers available and help you assess them.

"In your discussions with lenders, it helps to understand how they are thinking. Lenders must answer this question: will this business be successful?"

When a lender considers you as a prospective purchaser they will first assess your business proposal and then interview you. Two factors are of supreme importance: your quality as an applicant and the viability of the business you propose to purchase.

When lenders consider a loan application, they need to see relevant experience on the part of the purchaser and evidence of their achievements. Although it helps to have direct experience of the market sector you are proposing to move into, banks will consider experience in other relevant areas such as marketing, public relations and accountancy. This is where you must use your well-prepared CV (see Chapter 2, pages 39–41). They need to know that they can trust you with their money. Banks look for energy, creativity and drive. If you have these qualities in abundance, it will show in your CV and in your Business Plan.

The next stage is assessing the viability of the business. All the knowledge you gain in researching the business sector and the specific business you want to buy can be used to great effect here.

Lenders take into account many factors, such as various ratios (borrowing against the value of the business), the equity you are investing in the business, an assessment of the business's previous accounts, the tenure of the property and your development plans.

You will be expected to provide a historic record of how the business has traded over the past three years through Profit and Loss. In general, lenders are not interested in the Balance Sheet (unless you are buying a company). What they want to see is the profit figure before interest, tax and depreciation.

> "You should always under-promise and over-deliver because there is nothing banks like less than unrealistic objectives."

They will also want to analyse your forecasts for the next three years' trading, including injections of capital for new facilities and the upkeep of the building. You should always under-promise and over-deliver because there is nothing banks like less than unrealistic objectives. They will also expect to see capital investment built into your Business Plan in order to maintain the fabric of the business.

If you and your Business Plan succeed in passing the close scrutiny of the lender, the final stage is a personal interview. As in any interview, it is important that the lender likes you – and that includes the way you look. Banks, like other interviewers, are impressed by smartly dressed applicants with firm handshakes and good eye-to-eye contact.

Good interview technique will take you a long way. After meeting you and reviewing your application the lender may make a formal offer. If you accept, the money will be made available to you. It may be that the lender will require you to meet certain specific conditions. (See pages 76–7).

Business Plan and Financial Information

Business Plan

A Business Plan will help you set objectives and meet them, steer and manage the business, and be prepared for the future. It is vital to have one when you come to talk to your broker. Every Business Plan must include Financial Information which details the financial aspects of the business and includes essential figures such as turnover, profit and loss and cash flow. Financial Information should include a Cash Flow Plan and a Balance Sheet (see pages 63–6).

The rationale for a Business Plan is that it ensures you are clear about the purpose and running of your business. Assuming you have reached the stage where you are raising money and about to buy a business, it is worth planning exactly what that business will be doing over the next months and years. Many lenders require you to draw up a Business Plan as one of the supporting documents for a loan application. There is plenty of advice available on compiling and writing one.[5] Although this may all look daunting, there are good reasons for doing it:

> *"A Business Plan will help you set objectives and meet them, steer and manage the business, and be prepared for the future."*

- You need to show your lender and partners that you have thought about all aspects of the venture.
- The more work you do now, the fewer surprises you will have when you are running the business.
- The discipline of planning and structuring your venture will be vital in operating the business and in selling the idea to investors.
- You can use the Business Plan to build your business by attracting more investors and high-quality staff and managers.

While there is no accepted formula, a Business Plan needs to include the following in a clear structure:

- *A summary* – this outlines all the key elements of the Business Plan.
- *What this business is* – this should answer questions such as what stage is it at? What stage is the sector/industry at? What are the trends in the relevant part of the industry? What is unusual or unique about it? What are its Unique Selling Propositions (USPs) – in other words, what does it offer that no rival business offers? What are its strengths and weaknesses, opportunities and threats? What is the future of this business? Detail how you will stay in touch with developments in the industry – by using trade journals, trade shows, training courses and so on.
- *Your development plans* – detail the ways in which you plan to develop the business – for example, by extending the property, renovating, adding new services or new product ranges.
- *The locality and location* – describe where the business is and how this affects its trade, given that the more you rely on walk-in trade or on destination trade, the more important location is. Outline access, parking and any scope for further building or development (see Chapter 1, pages 23–25).
- *The property* – detail any leases or agreements that are in place; describe the buildings and the fabric; outline any restrictions that are in force.
- *The market* – explain who will use your service and why, outlining any benefits you can bring to your customers or clients. The gap between a product and a service is narrowing; be aware that you may well be offering both. Explain carefully how you will meet a need that your competitors do not.
- *The competition* – list your immediate competitors by market and location, describe their strengths

and weaknesses and estimate where your stiffest competition will come from. Then list your indirect competition by market and location (if appropriate). Detail your policy if these competitors threaten to take your market share. Outline how your product or service is better than that of your competitors.

- *Set-up, refurbishment and expansion* – detail the costs of setting up or refurbishing the business. Outline those areas of the business that you plan to expand and over what period. Specify the areas in which you can add value or develop new products and services.

> *"List your immediate competitors by market and location, describe their strengths and weaknesses and estimate where your stiffest competition will come from."*

- *Sales and marketing* – explain how you fit into both the overall and local markets; show how you will advertise and promote your business so that customers or clients know they need your service. A good Marketing Plan identifies your target audiences and assesses the means by which you can reach them – public relations, direct mail, e-mail marketing, advertising, promotion.

- *Management* – explain how the business is run, whether there are specialist staff, the hours the business opens, any legal constraints on the business. State how much time you and your family will be putting into the business.

- *Staffing and resources* – assess how many staff you need to employ and calculate your staffing costs. Who are the important staff, managers or advisors? List all the people who work in the business and their jobs, terms of employment and specific skills. List also any contracts that you must honour under legislation covered by the Transfer of Undertakings of Protection of Employment (TUPE) (see Appendix 1, page 204). Assess the cost of any possible re-structuring of the staff that you think you might need to make. You should include provision for possible claims for unfair dismissal. Bear in mind that if the re-structuring includes new employment terms, these may be ineffective in law if the reason for them is the transfer of the business.

> "Assess the cost of any possible re-structuring of the staff that you think you might need to make. You should include provision for possible claims for unfair dismissal."

- *Information technology, EPoS and stock control* – what IT systems are already in place in the business? Does the business use EPoS (electronic point of sale) and how does it currently monitor stock? Are you planning to update or make any changes to the current systems and, if so, how much capital will this require?

- *Risks* – state what could go wrong and why, and what the major liabilities of the business are (loans, wages, rent). Set out what insurance and indemnity you have to cover the business.

- *Pricing strategy* – list any suppliers and show how long it takes for any product or service to be brought to the point of sale. List your prices relative to those of your competitors and your tactics for dealing with price changes they might make. Note the impact of any change in government or EU duties or taxes. Draw up a sample price list for typical services and goods. Show how and where you make a profit. For this you will need to have drawn up Financial Information, a Cash Flow Plan and a Balance Sheet (see pages 63–6).

- *Agreements and approvals* – list any leases, licences, franchise agreements and EU, government or Local Authority approvals that may be required. If there are likely changes in any of these, state that.

- *How the business is operated* – you should also explain how your business is conducted, and how money is collected. How much paperwork is involved? Is your product or service based on capital, materials or on labour? Will this situation change over the next five years?

Financial Information, Cash Flow and Balance Sheet

Financial Information is related to the Business Plan but can stand alone. In it you set out all the financial data relevant to the business. There is no formula for Financial Information, but you must include the following:

- How much money is needed to buy, re-fit or expand the business.
- Where the funding comes from.
- How the business borrowing is arranged.
- The borrowing costs.
- The turnover and projected turnover.
- The projected costs.
- The projected profits.
- Turnover of stock or "churn".

Your plan will help you deal honestly and openly with the bank manager, any investors you may have, your customers, your suppliers and your staff. Of course, you need not show the documents to all of them, but knowing what targets and commitments you have will

> *"Your plan will help you deal honestly and openly with the bank manager, any investors you may have, your customers, your suppliers and your staff."*

help you to be clear about what you want from staff, suppliers and creditors and what you can promise to give them.

A Cash Flow Plan and Balance Sheet are essential if you are hoping to borrow money. While they are short documents, they represent a great deal of analysis and calculation. Together with the Financial Information, they answer the questions a lender might ask you, such as how you are planning to finance the business. The answers to this are in the Financial Information. A second question is what your incomings and outgoings are and when. The answers to this are in the Cash Flow. Thirdly, what money does the business have, and what does it owe or need to owe? The answers to this are in the Balance Sheet.

Financial Information

State how much money you will need now and over the next three to five years as capital. You may have raised money from equity in your home, or from life insurance policies, redundancy compensation or even against a future pension; but you may need to borrow. If so, state what you are offering as security for the loan (it may be the actual property of the business) and how long you need to repay it. Some businesses that fail do so because their owners either miscalculate how much they are able to borrow or they borrow too much and fail to take account of the variable cost of borrowing. Others forget to include future refurbishment and maintenance costs.

> *"Some businesses that fail do so because their owners either miscalculate how much they are able to borrow or they borrow too much..."*

Outline any specific lease, freehold or rental arrangements the business has in place.

Detail any tax advantages, EU, government or Local Authority subsidy, grant or loan that the business might attract.

State the predicted turnover of the business, the costs of the business (including staffing, utilities, goods and services bought in and insurance) and express them as a percentage of turnover. You should express turnover and predicted profits as ratios common to the sector in which you are buying your business (see "Key ratios" at the end of this chapter and of each sector chapter).

If you are buying a hotel or a care home, state the current and predicted levels of occupancy. Set out the number of rooms or bed spaces. If you are buying a restaurant, state the current and predicted number of covers. Give information about the trading areas – those parts of the property where the business is conducted, excluding owner's and staff accommodation, storage areas, offices and so on.

Cash Flow Plan

Some businesses fail because they do not regularly calculate their cash flow. A Cash Flow Plan gives you a series of projections for the sales (the money you collect) and expenditure (the money you pay out) of your business. This plan need not be complex, and it may be determined by the current performance of the business that you are proposing to buy. All you have to do, based on information you already have or on predictions you make, is to outline the cash coming in and the cash going out of the business each month for a year. Use a computerised spreadsheet program or simply draw up a large sheet of paper with 12 monthly columns along the top and a list of categories of income and expenditure down the side. Take account of contingencies and consider the best case/worst case scenarios. Allow for any temporary setbacks.

Balance Sheet

A Balance Sheet can be drawn up at any time, and should be done at least yearly. It shows the position of a business based on the actual accounts on a given day. A large company annual report is essentially a Balance Sheet. It includes what the business owns and what it owes, its assets and liabilities. These, in turn, are divided into current assets and liabilities and fixed assets and liabilities. Fixed assets are generally property, leases, plant, fixtures and fittings; fixed liabilities are long-term loans or debts which must be repaid over a long period. Current assets are the value of any stock in hand, the money in the bank, and anything owed by customers or clients. (There is a sub category called *quick assets*, which are essentially ready money.) Current liabilities are short-term debts, immediate bills and wages. The questions that arise immediately are simple and fundamental ones. Can the business pay its creditors if it sells its assets? Can the business meet its current liabilities from its current assets?

> *"The questions that arise immediately are simple and fundamental ones. Can the business pay its creditors if it sells its assets?"*

The relationship between fixed liabilities and fixed assets, current liabilities and current assets, and current liabilities and quick assets can be expressed as a ratio, and this will vary from business to business. An accountant who knows the business sector will have a clear sense of what is usual and what looks unusual.

Conclusion

The final element in your Business Plan is simply a section detailing any other material supporting your claims and credibility. This might include the following:

- Maps of the location.
- Pictures of the property, outside and inside.
- Local Authority structure plans.
- Demographic information.
- Personal references and CVs.
- Draft brochures and sample advertising.
- Architect's plans for expansion or rebuilding.
- Sample menus (restaurants), activity schedules

(care homes and children's day nurseries), daily specials (pubs).

- Proposed marketing strategy.
- Compliance with relevant legislation, for example Minimum Standards in care homes (see Chapter 10 and Appendix 1).
- Licensing requirements and your qualifications to meet these, if you have any, (see Appendix 1, pages 205–10).

Professional advice

You will need the services of a solicitor (lawyer) and an accountant as you begin your business. You should be clear about what you need from your lawyer. Make sure you know their hourly rates (many professional firms now bill in increments of six minutes), and keep a clear check on costs. The same applies to your accountant. Remember that those with experience of your chosen sector bring added expertise.

> *"Make sure you know their hourly rates (many professional firms now bill in increments of six minutes), and keep a clear check on costs."*

The more specific you can be about the type of advice you need, the faster and cheaper will be your contact with these two professions. Always use written instructions, and always set a limit on how much money can be spent at any one time in fees. When that limit is reached, have the solicitor or accountant write to you for further authorisation. Where you can, use standard forms and contracts for suppliers and employees. Use a lawyer to do the following:

- Form the legal entity which you trade under.
- Draw up your legal terms of trading.
- Convey the business purchase or lease.
- Draw up or check employment contracts for staff.
- Deal with day-to-day legal matters as they arise.

Use an accountant to do the following:

- Help draw up your Business Plan.
- Handle your VAT and personal and corporation tax returns.
- Deal with Companies House requirements for limited companies (if appropriate).
- Carry out the company audit (if appropriate).
- Plan for tax.

> *"Do not be intimidated by professional jargon – anyone who is intelligent should be able to explain an issue in clear English."*

Consultation with either a solicitor or an accountant may, for various reasons, be a point at which your business-buying process is delayed. Before you commit to a professional to help you, make sure that you have a similar style of conducting business – or at least that they recognise what yours is and respect it; make sure that you review the relationship periodically and let them know you are going to do so; and do not be intimidated by professional jargon – anyone who is intelligent should be able to explain an issue in clear English.

Key ratios

- *Loan-to-Value Ratio* – this is the ratio of what you are borrowing against the value of the business. Commercial lenders usually lend up to 75% (without additional security).
- *Interest Rate Cover Ratio* – this is the number of times the business's profits cover the annual interest. Lenders may require that a business must always have a cover ratio of, say, twice the borrowing costs.

Notes

1. Use business agents to put you in touch. A good source of information on business mortgages is www.christiefirst.com

2. See the *British Venture Capital Association Directory of Members*, published annually.

3. There are around 8,000 business angels in the UK with £500 million in investments. You can find them through your local Learning + Skills Council.

4. See *Financing Your Business*, Department of Trade and Industry, (DTI 98/805) and *Setting Up in Business* (DTI 01/725).

5. Examples include *The Small Business Handbook* by P and S Webb (Financial Times, 1999); the *Which Guide to Starting Your Own Business* (Which Books, 1999).

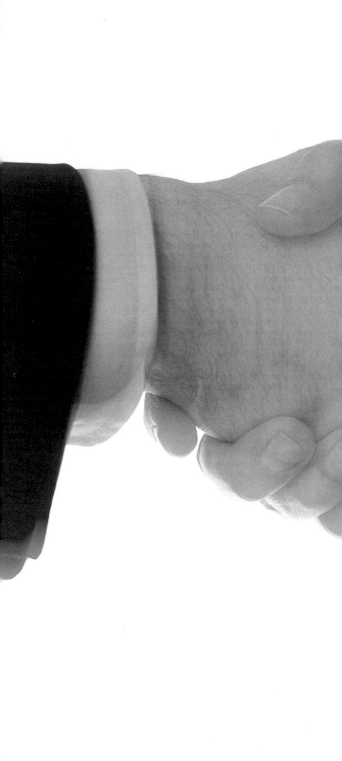

four

Buying
the business

This chapter introduces you to negotiating and making an offer. It looks at exchanging contracts and preparing both an inventory and a stock-take. It also covers finalising your finances, expenses, moving, insurance, pensions and investments.

Negotiating

Once you have looked over the business and are satisfied with the survey and the valuation, studied the competition and completed your market research in the area and, most importantly, examined and understood the accounts, you are ready to make an offer. There are no rules here, but there are plenty of negotiating styles, from the no-holds-barred negotiating style of City dealmakers to the collaborative style of those in long-term partnerships and alliances.

> *"Remember that any sensible vendor will have prepared the business ready for sale, if they have had time and opportunity."*

Always put yourself in the vendor's position. Remember that any sensible vendor will have prepared the business ready for sale, if they have had time and opportunity. This means that an intelligent vendor, acting prudently, has probably already done the following:

- Improved the sustainable profits of the business by cutting out excess costs and excessive salaries.
- Dealt with or made clear the costs in readiness for an incoming owner.
- Made moves to retain any managers or key staff for the business.
- Sought commitments from regular customers and suppliers.
- Made sure the building looks its best. Remember when looking at the building that the business is the most important aspect in the make-up of the over-

all value – a good business will pay its way, a poor one will struggle, no matter how good the building from which it operates.

Think about how many of these the vendor has done. But remember that the vendor can only have improved things to the best of his abilities. You will begin to build up a picture of the vendor's character and the best way of doing business with them.

As with most purchases, time is an element. Many good businesses sell quickly and locally, by word of mouth. There may be other buyers wanting to buy the business, and there may be little time for all the research that you want to do. Of course, it is no bad thing that other people should be interested, but this may drive up the purchase price or put pressure on you to move more quickly than you wish. Don't be hurried into making hasty decisions; there is always another business to buy if this one doesn't work out.

> *"Don't be hurried into making hasty decisions; there is always another business to buy if this one doesn't work out."*

By far the most important thing you can do before you negotiate is to prepare your case by asking some simple questions:[1] (see page 81)

- What do we want?
- What do they want?
- What are our strengths and weaknesses?
- What are their strengths and weaknesses?
- What are our principles here?
- What are we likely to disagree over?
- At what point do we cut off negotiations?
- What if this negotiation fails?
- What is our best alternative to a negotiated settlement?
- What is the maximum price we are prepared to pay for this business?

Here are some negotiating guidelines:

- Decide what you want and how much you will pay for it. This is distinct from how much you *can* pay, and is based on your Business Plan and Financial Information.
- Do not be pressured, embarrassed, flattered or duped into paying more than you think the business is worth.
- Always give your reasons for what you say and do.
- Try to explain your principles and relate your behaviour to them.
- Remember that enduring business relationships depend on trust.
- When you are honest, it is easier to be consistent.
- Always separate the people from the issues; that means you should never allow things to become personal.
- On the one hand, you want the best deal – but you should be careful not to upset the vendors, since you may need their help in the early stages of taking over the business. On the other hand, you should not be afraid to be tough.
- In a good deal, everyone wins.

> *"Do not be pressured, embarrassed, flattered or duped into paying more than you think the business is worth."*

Making your offer

When you decide to make an offer, you make it through the vendor's agent. Your offer will cover the purchase of the freehold or leasehold interests, the fixtures and fittings, and the goodwill (see Appendix 3, pages 223–4) of the business.[2] Tell your solicitor about your offer, and send it to the agent in writing. You may, at the time the offer is accepted, ask the vendor to remove the business from the market.

Your offer may be accepted or it may be rejected, and

you may find yourself in further negotiations. There may be a counter-offer from another potential purchaser. At this point you have to decide whether you want to continue negotiating yourself, and you need to find out whether the vendor plans to carry on negotiating with you. It is easy enough to be aggressive and play hard ball in your negotiations but remember, you may need the vendor's help and guidance in the future in ways and on matters you cannot predict.

Exchange of contracts and completion

If your offer is accepted, you should instruct your solicitor to be ready to receive (from the vendor's solicitor) a contract for the purchase. You will need to sign this contract and your solicitor can then exchange it with that signed by the vendor and held by his solicitor. These contracts are relatively simple and cover the fact that once a deposit is paid for the building it becomes the property of the purchaser, who must then insure it.[3] There may be various licences and permissions to transfer along with the business: restaurant and pub/bar licences, health and safety

> *"As part of the contract of sale, you will fix a date on which you will pay the remainder of the agreed price and the vendor will hand over the business."*

permissions and so on. As part of the contract of sale, you will fix a date on which you will pay the remainder of the agreed price and the vendor will hand over the business. Solicitors call this *completion*.

Inventory and stocktake

Before contracts are exchanged, an inventory should be prepared. This should be drawn up by an inventory specialist[4] and checked on the day of completion. It should list all the fixtures and fittings included in the sale and show those items that are subject to hire purchase, leasing, rental or on free loan from product suppliers (eg ice cream fridges, coffee machines). If something is not specified in the list of items for sale, do not assume it will remain with the business – examples are garden furniture, statues and paintings on the walls. If you have any doubts about a particular item, ask if it is to be removed. If it is not, make sure it is included in the list of items for sale. The stock and goods that will enable you to continue trading should be valued on the day of completion by a specialist stocktaker[5]. This is called a stocktake and the figure produced is known as *Stock at Valuation* or SAV.

> "The broker will co-ordinate the information that you need to finalise your loan application. They will also have identified your lender..."

Finalising your finances

This is the point in the buying process where you will benefit from a good relationship with a dependable broker or business mortgage specialist. Your early conversations with them – or with any lender – should have fixed your budget. Now you need their help to see you through the final stages of the buying process. By this stage, a good broker will have done several things:

- Listed the information a lender needs.
- Co-ordinated with the valuers who are producing the Valuation Report.
- Made formal representations to the lender and provided you with details of the range of loans available, and of matters such as redemption penalties, personal guarantees and life cover.
- Worked with your solicitor and accountant to make sure that your purchase moves forward smoothly.

The broker will co-ordinate the information that you need to finalise your loan application. They will also have identified your lender and presented the lender with the following:

- Business Plan and Financial Information.
- Personal and professional references.
- Accounts from the existing business.
- Valuation Report and Structural Survey (see Appendix 3).
- Details of any security you can offer for the loan (usually assets you own).
- Your CV.

On the strength of this material, the lender will know a great deal about you and the business you are proposing to buy. After interviewing you and reviewing your application, the lender can make a formal offer. The money should be made available to you via your business's bank account,

> *'Remember that you may have other borrowing expenses connected with the business, such as hire purchase or equipment leasing."*

enabling you to go ahead and buy your business. Make sure you ask your lender how the money is to be transferred to your account and that you know how you are going to transfer it to either the vendor's or their solicitor's account on the day you complete the purchase. Remember that you may have other borrowing expenses connected with the business, such as hire purchase or equipment leasing.

Expenses

During this phase of buying your business, you must pay your solicitor and your accountant, and you must pay any stamp duty at the prevailing rate and any loan arrangement fees. If you are selling any property to finance the business – such as your family home or another business – you will have a further set of professional fees to pay.[6] At the same time you need to plan for your personal and business expenses connected with the physical moving and transfer of the business.

There may be refurbishments and alterations to be done before you can move into the owner's accommodation and this, of course, must be carefully planned and included in your budget. There may also be removal expenses and additional costs relating to overnight accommodation, childcare, and kennels for pets on the day of the move.

Moving

Moving house or taking possession of a new business is a matter of being organised and calm. There is plenty of removal advice available, either from local removal firms or on the Internet.[7] As you approach your moving date, make sure that you know what you will be doing about the following, if appropriate:

- *Children* – have them looked after elsewhere on the day of the move.
- *Pets* – send them to kennels, if necessary.
- *Packing and labelling* – bear in mind that last in will be first out of the container and/or removal van.
- *School registration* – for your children.
- *Taking some time off work* – to manage your move.
- List things you are taking with you.
- Give away things you don't need.
- Notify anyone who needs to know your change of address, including utilities.
- Set up a mail-forwarding service from your old address.

Insurance

One of the most important aspects of buying your own business is insuring it against the wide variety of risks. It might be a good idea to discuss your insurance requirements with a reputable insurance broker.[8]

- *Buildings* – you should insure the building against fire and flood. Most business owners fund their acquisition through a bank or lender. These will insist on adequate buildings insurance.
- *Trading Contents* – these comprise the fixtures and fittings of the business, together with the stock and equipment necessary to operate it. Such policies usually offer standard sums to cover certain levels of stock – for example wines and spirits, refrigerated and frozen foods and any money held on the premises.
- *Employer's Liability* – it is a legal requirement for businesses to insure their premises against any claims from employees resulting from accidents while working on the premises. The standard sum insured is £10 million.
- *Public Liability* – this is another legal requirement. It protects the business in the event of an accident or injury being sustained by any member of the public visiting the premises. In the case of hospitality businesses – as well as those in the retail and care sectors, which deal with the public – it is vital that the business has adequate insurance to cover any claims.

> *"...it is a legal requirement for businesses to insure their premises against any claims from employees resulting from accidents while working on the premises."*

- *Consequential Loss* – this is also known as Business Interruption or Loss of Profits insurance. It covers the business in the event of loss of profits as a consequence of an insured peril such as fire, flood or storm damage.
- *Fidelity* – this will cover you if staff are caught stealing from your business. Remember, it is possible to claim under some other policies for theft by

employees, provided that theft is detected within 14 days of its occurrence. However, as frauds are rarely detected within this period, you would be wise to have this type of insurance to cover the eventuality.

- *Key Staff* – you, your manager or your chef, for example, may be absolutely vital to the success of your business. You should protect your business in the event of the loss of a key member of the team. The reputation of a restaurant may depend on its chef, or the manager of a nursing home may be critical to its successful operation. This policy, which usually pays out a lump sum in the event of the death of a key employee, is particularly important in a partnership.

> **"You should protect your business in the event of the loss of a key member of the team. The reputation of a restaurant may depend on its chef, or the manager of a nursing home may be critical to its successful operation."**

- *Personal Accident* – this is taken out by individuals, rather than a business, to ensure that their wages will be covered in the event of their being unable to work for up to 12 months. You may wish to consider this type of insurance to protect your own income.

- *Income Protection Plan* – this is not as common as it used to be. Unlike Personal Accident, it pays out to the company in the event of an employee falling sick and being unable to work. However, many businesses these days decide to "self insure" – in other words, to pay out of their own reserves rather than pay monthly premiums.

Pensions and investments

Your financial planning should include provision for pension and investment funds. It is mandatory for businesses employing five or more staff – including part-time as well as full-time – to offer employees the option of a stakeholder pension. Your broker, lender or the business's bank will be able to discuss details and appropriate schemes with you.

Notes

1. One of the best negotiating guides is *Getting to Yes* by William Ury and Roger Fry, 1997; see also their *Getting Past No*, 1997. Other useful guides are: *The Perfect Negotiation* by Gavin Kennedy, 1999; *Pocket Negotiator* by Gavin Kennedy, (*Economist*, 2001); *The Art and Science of Negotiation* by Howard Raiffa, 1990.

2. There may be some adjustment in the price to take account of liability for stamp duty, which is paid by the purchaser on the building. Negotiate this if you can.

3. There are specialist insurers who will draw up policies to cover the buildings and the cost of reinstating them (not necessarily their value), employer's liability, public liability, business contents, loss of profits, loss of licence and cash.

4. and 5. See Venners (stocktakers and inventory specialists): www.venners.com

6. Examples are Local Search Fee, Land Registry Search Fee, Land Registration Fee, banking costs for transferring funds.

7. For example, www.ihavemoved.com

8. See Christie First at www.christiefirst.com

Summary of Essentials from Chapters 1–4

What kind of business and how much can you afford?	How do you find the right business?	Is it a business worth buying?	How do you buy it?
Look at advertisements with the biggest choice in the trade, regional and national press.	Talk to agents, read local and trade press, use the Internet.	View the business and discuss it with a broker or agent.	Set out a timetable, take advice on the pitfalls and legal implications, trade requirements and regulations.
Talk to business mortgage specialists. Discuss your financial position and price range, etc.	Ensure that you can afford to buy a particular business, before viewing.		Explore financing options with a business mortgage specialist. Secure a loan. Effect any necessary insurance cover.
		Appraise the potential and value of the business.	
		Obtain feasibility study. Produce cash flow forecasts.	Obtain listing and valuation of fixtures and fittings. Accurate stocktaking on completion.

How can you ensure it is a success?	How do you ensure it runs efficiently?	Once it is a success, what are your options?	Whom do you contact?
	Take advice on rates and rent reviews.	Utilise service to target further acquisitions.	Business agent.
Plan for your future prosperity. Look at business and personal insurance. Discuss pensions and financial planning.		Plan for growth through expansion, acquisition or selling. Look at re-mortgages, and get your tax planning organised. Plan for your retirement. Utilise your equity to expand.	Business finance broker.
Carry out detailed financial appraisal.			Business valuer.
On-going stocktaking. Review systems.	Make sure your bookkeeping is kept accurate and up to date.	Talk to a professional specialist management consultant about business development.	Business valuer and stocktaker.

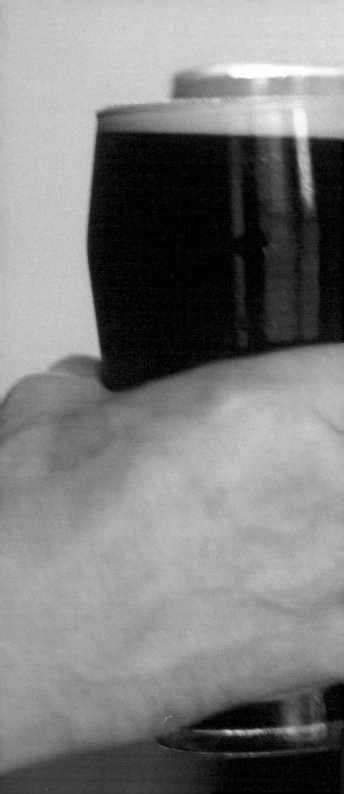

five

How to
buy a pub

A n introduction to the pub sector. Are you the right person to run a pub? What kind of pub do you want and where? Managed, tenancy, lease or freehouse? Finding a pub. Is this the right pub for you? Reading pub accounts. Improving the business.

An introduction to the pub sector

The British pub is a long-established part of our social and economic life, a magnet for tourists, the hub of village and rural life and a focal point for young and old alike. There are approximately 60,000 pubs in the UK, providing food and drink to varying degrees. As our leisure needs and wants have changed, so too have our pubs. These days pubs often have restaurants as well as serving snack meals at the bar. Many also offer accommodation and facilities for private functions such as weddings, dinners and club or association events. The last decade of the 1900s saw dramatic changes sweeping through the pub sector as national brewers increasingly sold their pub estates, predominantly to the fast-growing pub-operating companies. In turn, these chains continue to rationalise their pub portfolios, selling on those that no longer fit their strategy. As a result, independent pub operators and aspiring first-time buyers are able to choose from a wide variety of pub properties which are reverting once again to freehouses.

> *"This continual flux in the market means there is usually a plentiful supply of good-quality pubs for sale."*

The British Beer & Pub Association (formerly The Brewers and Licensed Retailers Association) has issued figures showing that certain kinds of pubs – predominantly rural and suburban – are closing at the rate of around 400 per year, but that urban pubs are opening at around the same rate. This continual flux in the market means there is usually a plentiful supply of good-quality pubs for sale.

Pubs, restaurants and hotels – known collectively as the licensed trades – can provide attractive returns of between 10% and 20% on capital invested in freehold properties. (See Appendix 2 for the differences between freehold and leasehold.) Leasehold properties can provide returns of between 20% and 50%, but it should be remembered that the asset is not necessarily appreciating in value. As property prices fluctuate, so do the prices of property-related businesses like those in the licensed trades. For those who live in their investment, as live-in landlords, this fluctuation is much the same as they

> *"Leasehold properties can provide returns of between 20% and 50%, but it should be remembered that the asset is not necessarily appreciating in value."*

might experience in a private home. The price of a business, of course, also fluctuates as profits increase or decrease and as markets wax and wane in tune with national and world economies. But, as with residential property, most people make a gain in capital value.

Are you the right person to run a pub?

People decide to buy and run a pub for many reasons. For some it is a matter of business, for others a matter of lifestyle. For many there is a combination of a number of factors. Many first-time buyers have a sense of the market as a consumer; we all know what we like in a pub, hotel or restaurant.

The first place to start your research is with yourself. What kind of person are you really? Are you sure you are suited to running a pub? Ask yourself the following questions:

- Do you really like and enjoy people?

- Can you relate to a wide range of classes, occupations, shapes and sizes?
- Are you judgemental?
- Are you committed and eager to let people know your views?
- Can you keep secrets and are you comfortable with gossip?
- Do you mind being an authority figure?
- Are you happy to work hard and to work unsocial hours?

Be clear about what you like and dislike, what you know and what you don't; where you are strong and where you are weak, and where your practical and social skills lie. You are the biggest part of the investment you are about to make, and you need to know yourself thoroughly (see Chapter 2, pages 38–9).

Running a pub as a resident licensee can be demanding, both mentally and physically. The hours are long, there is little scope for time off, and the pub itself has to be open when most other people are not working – most pubs need to be open from 11 am to 11 pm seven days a week, every week of the year. When the licensing laws are eventually changed, opening hours are likely to be relaxed, meaning even longer hours for the publican. Anyone who has worked in a pub – behind the bar, at tables or in the kitchen – knows it is hard work. If you have never worked in a pub, it may be a good idea to get a job to see from the inside what the working life can be like. Talk to your local publican too.

> **"Be clear about what you like and dislike, what you know and what you don't; where you are strong and where you are weak..."**

Successful pubs are invariably run by good, established partnerships – of whatever make-up. The key to running a pub successfully as a partnership is that the partners must be committed to the success of the business, whatever roles they take on. Any relationship can suffer the strain of long hours and hard work, particularly in the rough-and-tumble environment behind some bars. In fact, pub companies stress the importance of compatible couples to run their pubs because they know that will help commercial success.

Training for the licensed trades is becoming increasingly important. A good training course should cover the business, social and legal aspects of running a pub. The National Licensee's Certificate, though not compulsory, provides a good standard of knowledge across a range of licensing issues including justices' licences, hours, young people, employment, weights and measures, notices, social responsibilities of the licensee and so on.[1] (See page 104.) The National Licensee's Certificate is offered by the British Institute of Innkeeping (BII), which co-ordinates courses for it across the UK. You are recommended to obtain this qualification before you apply to the licensing committee for your licence as the committee will recognise its value. The BII is a central source of information on training and licensing matters in general.

> *"Most pubs need to be open from 11 am to 11 pm seven days a week, every week of the year."*

What kind of pub do you want and where?

Once you have decided you would like to work in a pub, you can begin to look for the kind that would suit you best. As businesses, pubs and bars depend on their locality and location (see Chapter 1, pages 23–5); in fact, many are shaped and defined by where they are. So, the next thing you must think about is location. Most pubs fall into one of the following three broad categories:

- *Inner-city or town pub* – usually in the centre of town, reachable on foot, often on a town's "drinking circuit"; it might be a fashionable bar, a lunchtime place for office workers, or a popular and busy weekend spot.

- *Suburban pub* – often serving a local and passing community and often situated on the outskirts of town near a residential district; it may provide family facilities.
- *Country pub* – which many customers travel to rather than live near, known in the trade as a "destination pub". It may be in an area of outstanding beauty, or it may draw people with its range of food at country – rather than city – prices.

> *"It is likely that your pub will be your main investment, so you must proceed carefully and look for advice at every step."*

The search for the right pub for you is actually quite simple; it is a matter of fixing priorities. You may decide on the type of pub, or you may decide on the part of the country you want to move to. Either way, you should do as much preliminary reading, research and fact-gathering as you possibly can. It is likely that your pub will be your main investment, so you must proceed carefully and look for advice at every step.

Each of the three pub types described previously has its distinct character and qualities, and each is governed by clear economics relating to a dizzying variety of variables such as space, location, clientele, reputation and so on. Every pub has competition. Wherever it is, it is vital to know the neighbourhood and character of the competition – who they are, where they are and what they are offering that you could do better.

Here are a few of the most important questions you need to ask about any pub:

- Are there any captive markets – offices, residential blocks of flats and so on?

- Is there space to expand?
- Is the pub or bar open all day?
- Could the turnover be increased through non-alcoholic sales – for instance, by increasing the sale of food or adding accommodation?
- Is it a fashionable "theme bar" that may go out of fashion?
- What are the social profiles of its customers?
- What ages are the customers and where do they come from?
- How much does each person spend on average?
- What might improve this pub?
- Is this a family pub?
- Where are the profits mainly coming from?
- What is the competition, either locally (for a town centre or suburban pub) or within 20–30 minutes' drive (for a destination pub)?
- What makes this pub distinctive?
- Does the pub's reputation depend on one chef or one owner/manager?
- Does the pub cater for outside events, for example parties, weddings and conferences?

Of course, not all pubs fit neatly into any particular category. In emerging and changing markets, hybrid businesses evolve to meet the changing needs of the public. The surest tactic in a changing environment is to add to and develop the skills, goods and services you offer.

> *"Ask yourself where you can develop and add value to your business. This will help you clarify your thinking about your market…"*

Ask yourself where you can develop and add value to your business. This will help you clarify your thinking about your market and what you are offering your customers. For example, could you do any of the following:

- Make better use of the garden?
- Add a separate restaurant area?
- Cater for and host meetings or events for local clubs and associations?
- Improve and extend the current menus or the selection of beers, lagers and wines?
- Host parties and quiz nights?
- Offer children's facilities; special offers for pensioners before 12.30 pm; speciality coffees, afternoon teas, bed and breakfast?
- Introduce new marketing ideas?

Managed, tenancy, lease or freehouse

Once you have settled on the type of pub and the type of business you wish to attract, you must consider the arrangement that will suit you best. There are four ways in which a pub is run: managed, tenancy, lease and freehouse. How a pub is run is distinct from how it is owned.

> *"Entering the industry as the manager of a pub is the cheapest course; however, you will be an employee... rather than your own boss."*

A freehouse is not necessarily a freehold. No one option is essentially any better than another in terms of the profits to be made. Tenancies, for example, can be highly profitable while a freehouse can sometimes be less so. However, a freehouse tends to have a higher value. One way of thinking about these four categories is the level of investment that they represent relative to the size of the business obtained and the money you will need if you wish to buy into the industry.

Managed

Over a third of the country's pubs are managed houses. These are pubs owned by breweries and pub companies ("multiples" or "pubcos") and they include theme bars, branded pubs and steak houses. The managers are trained by the company or brewery and are employed on a fixed salary with a bonus scheme, and they do not own the business. The operating company is responsible for all the operating costs, any refurbishment costs and any capital outgoings. There is plenty of support, training, advice and professional back-up, particularly from the larger multiples. The average managed house turnover (excluding VAT) is £8,000–£10,000 a week, although in some companies there is a much higher average turnover than this. To become the publican of a managed house you need no greater investment than a security bond (usually under £5,000), which many pub companies require. Entering the industry as the manager of a pub is the cheapest course; however, you will be an employee of the company, rather than your own boss.

Tenancy

These customarily take the form of a tied tenancy, a short-term agreement in which the tenant rents the

> "The tenant pays for all the running expenses of the pub together with some repairs and decoration, usually internal only. Any profit and loss falls to the tenant."

pub subject to a tie (an agreement to buy beer and related products from the landlord). The landlord profits from the rent, the returns on the sale of its products and any discounts it receives from suppliers. The tenant pays for all the running expenses of the pub together with some repairs and decoration, usually internal only. Any profit and loss falls to the tenant. Following a government investigation of the pub sector in 1989, national breweries generally gave up offering traditional tenancies. In their place, pub companies were set up to run chains of pubs under tied tenancy. While these pub companies are not brewers, a tied tenancy from one of them is not dissimilar from a traditional tied tenancy because the pub companies themselves all have trading agreements with one or more brewer. The weekly turnover is up to £6,000, possibly more. The cost of entry is usually between £10,000 and £35,000; the tenant buys the fixtures and fittings and all the stock but does not have to commit any more capital.

Lease

These were introduced in 1988 after Grand Metropolitan, a leading UK drinks company, created the Inntrepreneur 20-year lease. Generally, there is a tie for beer although there may be a provision to offer one guest beer (real ale). Under typical terms, the lessee keeps the profits, bears the losses and can sell the business (but not the property) for whatever it is worth (its premium value). This will depend on profitability, the number of years of the lease remaining and the value of the fixtures and fittings, plus stock at valuation. You can purchase an existing lease with the benefit of goodwill and trading accounts at a premium. Alternatively, multiples and pubcos grant new leases, usually without a premium. After freehouses, purchasing a lease is the most expensive way of entering the pub trade, usually costing from £40,000 to £100,000 or more.

> *"...you can purchase an existing lease with the benefit of goodwill and trading accounts at a premium."*

Freehouse (leasehold or freehold)

Freehouse describes how the business is run (ie without a tie); freehold or leasehold describes how it is owned. Around a third of all pubs are owned outright by the licensee. Traditionally, most rural pubs are in this category; and some urban pubs and bars are held freehold. The freehouse licensee has the freedom to choose suppliers. The freeholder can lease out the pub in due course (see Tenancy and Lease above) run it under new management, or sell. A freehold freehouse is usually the most flexible and secure kind of ownership. The average freehouse turnover is £4,000–£6,000 a week (excluding VAT). To buy a freehold pub you have to pay for everything including the property and the goodwill of the business.

This is the most expensive form of entry into the pub trade. A freehold can cost anything from £100,000.

Where to find what is available

Managed houses, tenancies, leases and freehouses are advertised in *The Morning Advertiser*, *The Publican*, *Daltons Weekly* and *Caterer & Hotelkeeper*. Many advertisements are placed by tenancy brokers acting on behalf of brewers and pub companies, and relate to tenancies and leases. Brokers take their fee from the ingoing tenant. Both freehouses and leases tend to be sold through specialist agencies and a wide variety of pubs is generally on offer throughout the country at any one time. Agents usually take their fee from the vendor and represent their interests. However, agents can be very useful to the buyer as they can be a good source of expertise and information. The longer their experience in the industry and the wider their geographical coverage, the better they can equate local conditions to national trends. You will find that the larger agents have harnessed information technology and invested in the worldwide web to make details of businesses they are handling widely available. As well as looking for national coverage, look for a web site that gives you up-to-date information about the businesses an agent has for sale.

> *"You will find that the larger agents have harnessed information technology and invested in the worldwide web to make details of businesses they are handling widely available."*

The agent and the price

When you come to buy a tenancy, lease or freehouse, matters can become quite complex, and you will need professional advice on legal, property and business aspects of your intended purchase. Remember, you are buying a business with all its related complexities. An agent is the obvious and best place to start, not only because they will have access to information and experience which you do not have, but also because they will have contacts with valuers, stocktakers, solicitors and specialist business finance brokers. While an agent representing the vendor may not seem to have your interests foremost in mind, it is certain that, in order to make the sale happen for the vendor, that agent will have to take a number of your concerns seriously. You may be buying a pub for the first time, so use their expertise and advice. They will certainly be aware that one day you may be a seller who may require their services.

"Why is this pub on the market? Ask the owners polite and direct questions to find out what their reasons for selling really are."

Clearly, the greatest determinant of price is the success of the business, and good, well-ordered premises with a strong customer base will always cost more than those which are not.

Is this the right pub for you?

After you have arranged your financing, prepared your Business Plan, undertaken background research and looked at lots of sales details sent to you by business agents, you will have a sense of what you like and what you can afford. You are now ready to view properties and select one you want to buy. Here are some of the questions you should consider as you narrow your search:

- Why is this pub on the market? Ask the owners polite and direct questions to find out what their reasons for selling really are. Listen to what is not said as carefully as to what is.

- How long have the owners been here?
- What was the pub like before the current owners bought it?
- Have these owners done all they can with the pub? This is an important question, simply because you need to look very carefully at the potential of the business and its ability to generate a good profit – before you commit to it. A busy, successful pub takes energy and ideas to manage; and a deserted, unsuccessful pub will take as much energy and money to change. Talk to the owners about their approach to the pub and about what they have tried to do over the last few years.

> *"A busy, successful pub takes energy and ideas to manage; and a deserted, unsuccessful pub will take as much energy and money to change."*

- What role does the publican have? This is a vital question. The landlord is often at the centre of local social life and you need to be aware of the role you will be expected to play.
- Is there a barman, chef or manager who is central to the business, or whose departure might damage it?
- Is the landlord simply a manager or investor who employs transient bar staff and has little or nothing to do with the day-to-day operation of the pub?

Reading pub accounts

Whether you are buying a freehouse or a lease, you should see and study the trading accounts. You should ask for Profit and Loss Accounts for three years, and require the vendor to show you the key data for the current one. You should also ask for details of specific incomes from gaming and other machines, outside catering, room hire, functions and so on, as appropriate.

However, some pubs sold by breweries/pub companies that have an incumbent tenant will have no accounts available as these will be the property of the tenant. In these circumstances you should ask for the last three years' barrelage figures, which will give an indication of recent levels of trading. Having looked at the accounts, you will want to make your own Financial Plan based on the data you gather from them. Accounts take many forms (see Chapter 1, pages 27–35).

> *'From the accounts it should be possible to see where the pub's profits come from, and to identify areas for further growth."*

From the accounts it should be possible to see where the pub's profits come from, and to identify areas for further growth. You should try to determine the following:

- What is the proportion of "wet sales" (drinks), food, accommodation and outside events? Can any of these be increased or decreased to produce more profit?
- What is the trading area of the property? How does this relate to turnover and to customer numbers at various times of the day, month or year?
- How much beer does the pub sell? This important figure, known as the *barrelage* (based on a notional standard barrel size of 36 gallons), has already been mentioned. Some people use the barrelage figure as a check, viewing the price of the pub as a multiple of the barrels sold.

Structural Survey and Valuation Report

It is important to have a Structural Survey and Valuation Report for the pub you want to buy (see Appendix 3). A competent Structural Survey concentrates on the detailed condition of the building and a Valuation

Report will cover the location, condition of the building, accommodation, services, planning, tenure, rates, fixtures and fittings, licences (see Appendix 1, pages 205–10), staffing[2] and goodwill.

Improving the business

During the 1990s and the first few years of the 2000s, the number of company-owned pubs grew to the extent that many managed pub chains became familiar across the country. An independent operator competing with what the multiples have to offer must always compete on price, quality and service. While the managers of multiples have to meet targets, maintain the brand values of the chain and adhere to strict stock control, the independent publican can move quickly and decide where to compete and when. The latter knows the local market, and can adjust stock, pricing, opening hours, staffing and almost any variable consistent with making a profit.

Your market research should have given you an idea of how your chosen pub trades at various times of day and at various times of the week, month and season. You should also have an idea of how well your potential competitors are trading. Remember that your competitors are not necessarily just other pubs, but also bars, cafés, restaurants, tourist centres and hotel bars. However, a pub's main competition comes from the following:

> *"Remember that your competitors are not necessarily just other pubs, but also bars, cafés, restaurants, tourist centres and hotel bars."*

- *Sport and leisure* – drinking at social venues other than pubs.
- *The home* – our homes are generally better and more comfortable than they were a generation ago, with fridges well-stocked with drink either bought

from supermarkets or off-licences, or imported cheaply from abroad.

Decide if there are services you can offer that your competitors cannot, and make plans to develop those services. The market you are competing for may be defined by location, class, wealth and lifestyle. Is there any particular service you can offer an interest group such as walkers, bikers, office workers, Internet users, sports groups or local associations?

Here are some of the ways in which publicans typically add value to their businesses by increasing turnover and profits.

Food

As habits change, food becomes increasingly important to the pub sector. It can account for up to 50% of turnover and sometimes has a higher profit margin than alcohol sales, depending on the pricing and the quality of the food. As an independent operator you have an advantage over the multiples because you can offer individuality and flexibility. However, you can look to the pub companies for ideas – for example, theme nights, different prices and times – and make them your own. Whatever you do, do it well. While you may not be able to source your produce and supplies as cheaply as a multiple, you have more control over what you do and how you do it.

> *"Keep the menu simple; you can use the same menu for lunch and evening meals, putting daily specials on a blackboard."*

Keep the menu simple; you can use the same menu for lunch and evening meals, putting daily specials on a blackboard. Fashions in food reflect the shape and tastes of society as a whole and your local community in particular. The most important food fashions are new and traditional British, European, Asian (Indian, Chinese and Thai), fusion cooking (created by mixing two or more ethnic cuisines), dishes for the health-conscious and organic. For faster food, look for ideas from commercial sandwich-makers, the multiples and fashionable hotels. Aim for gross profits (before any expenses) of between 50% and 70% on all your food sales.

See if you can fill a gap by offering brunch; all-day breakfast; pre-cinema, pre-theatre or pre-match meals; eat-early deals; speciality coffees; afternoon tea; menus for children; take-away sandwiches; barbecues and so on. You can often reach a new market by providing the same thing at a different time of day for a different price.

Wine

Add quality and variety, but avoid carrying too much expensive stock. A dozen wines sold by the bottle or glass are ample for most pubs. Use blackboard displays and rotate promotions on wines from around the world. Brief your staff on the wines without making them wine bores. Decide on a mark-up policy which encourages people to drink more expensive wines in bigger measures (standard measures are 12.5 cl and 17.5 cl).

Spirits

Know your market and keep pace with trends in drinking across the range of age groups. Do not stock too wide a range of spirits (probably just the two market leaders in each category), but do specialise in one area (eg whiskies, vodkas). Sell spirits using optics, which make the products attractive, displaying their own specific advert. Be aware of the power of eye-level displays, and take advice from a merchandising or display designer to make the most of what you have.

> *"Be aware of the power of eye-level displays, and take advice from a merchandising or display designer to make the most of what you have."*

Usually, the highest profits are to be made at the top end of the market.

Premium (Packaged) Lagers (PPLs) and special beers

These are really the range of top brands. An independent freehouse can stock a wide range and steal a march on the tied houses. The range might include bottled beer from Belgium, Germany, the UK and the USA and can be bolstered with beers from South America or Mexico. Read travel literature on the places your customers go to on holiday and find out about the new beers they might discover while abroad. Give information on blackboards and run regular promotions on beers worldwide.

> *"Read travel literature on the places your customers go to on holiday and find out about the new beers they might discover while abroad."*

Flavoured Alcoholic Beverages (FABs)

This range of drinks tends to appeal to certain drinkers but, like PPLs, they are subject to fashion and trends. However, they provide good opportunities as they are generally not included in any tie.

Entertainment

This can take many forms and is a vast subject, from bar games and live music to outdoor barbecues. In brief, you may need a different range of licences and permissions for various performances, dancing and even karaoke.

Marketing and publicity

This is normally one of the most important ways of promoting your pub to potential customers. You should have a Marketing Plan as part of your Business Plan. As you get to know the business, you will see which parts are weak and which are strong. You should have a clear idea of *who your customers are*, and why and when they come to your pub; and of *who your potential customers are,* and why and when they might come to your pub. Then you can match your existing and potential customers with the facilities you have or plan to have. As part of your marketing assessment, try to look objectively at the facilities already in the pub and also at the facilities you might want to add – examples are a garden area, a conservatory and a functions room – and then see if your competitors are offering anything similar. Try to offer something that no one else has. Once you have identified what you have to offer – your Unique Selling Proposition (USP) – you can publicise and market the business by talking to local journalists, getting into directories and listings and advertising your business. You should think about how to reach specific markets – such as women, students, "greys" (retired and older people) or "pinks" (the gay population) – with special promotions and offers. Retaining business is vital. Marketing professionals reckon it takes six times more effort to get a new customer than to retain an existing one. If the pub you buy is successful, think twice about whether you should change it.

> *"Marketing professionals reckon it takes six times more effort to get a new customer than to retain an existing one."*

Key ratios

- *Ratio of wet sales and food sales* – a wet-led pub will have 90–95% wet sales; whereas in a food-driven pub, food could account for 60–70% of sales.
- *Percentage of net profit to net turnover* – quite simply, the higher the percentage, the more successful the pub is. Some managed-house chains achieve in excess of 30% net profit to turnover.
- *Percentage of staff costs to turnover* – those pubs with high food sales will have a higher percentage of staff costs, probably from 20 to 30%, whereas wet-led pubs should be below this figure.

Top tips

- Don't rush into making changes; assess things first.
- Sell good-quality beer, served to customers through clean pipes.
- Hire, train and retain good, trustworthy staff.
- Make sure all areas, especially the toilets and the kitchens, are clean. Keep all public areas looking fresh. External appearance is vital for passing trade.
- Appoint a good stocktaker.
- Set up and maintain pub teams – for example darts – to sustain year-round trade.

Notes

1. See information available from the British Institute of Innkeeping.
2. Under legislation covered by the Transfer of Undertakings of Protection of Employment (TUPE), a new owner is obliged to transfer the current staff contracts under almost all circumstances (see Appendix 1).

pubs – a case study
Paul Emery: The Cross Keys, Todmorden

Paul Emery began his career in the public house trade in 1993 with just £950 and a Ford Escort van worth £800. A few months into the new millennium, this highly determined man, with a very clear vision of success, had acquired six pubs – all through Christie & Co. Having successfully managed the Cross Keys pub in Todmorden, West Yorkshire for a while, he convinced his bankers that he had the ideas, skill and sheer determination to justify a 100% loan to acquire the business. After buying the business, he re-built and extended it by buying the house next door.

He believes every square metre of the property must be made to generate revenue. "That's where most pub operators go wrong. In fact, I ran out of room at the pub and was even told I was over-trading." He sold the Cross Keys for four times what he paid for it – an excellent return on investment in that he was able to fund the purchase of other businesses from the pub's cash flow. "I have never sat on my money. I make £2 and I invest £4."

He specialises in taking over bankrupt, closed and even fire-damaged businesses, renovating them and turning them into high-turnover operations. He re-built another pub to create a good working-class beer house with a very high barrelage. When he bought a fire-damaged, Grade II Listed hotel and undertook a £1 million renovation, the project was bigger than he realised and nobody thought he would survive to finish it. He had over-stretched himself financially, but with determination and grit he pressed on with the works. His considerable self-belief got him through difficult times. In hindsight, he would do it differently, with more planning; he learned a lot about man-management skills, planning, organisation and shrewdness.

> "I could have had just two or three pubs and made a very nice living, but I am going for the super league."

Whilst others tremble at taking on a six-figure mortgage, Paul Emery said confidently: "In three months' time I hope to have a seven-figure mortgage backed by lots of assets. I could have had just two or three pubs and made a very nice living, but I am going for the super league." To some, he is already in the super league, anticipating an annual turnover of £2.5 million once all renovation work is complete and all his present five pubs are fully trading.

The pub sector has changed dramatically since the 1980s and Paul Emery believes those who are being left behind are the ones who won't change to keep up with market trends. He also knows that the only way to run a group of pubs successfully is to make sure that his staff understand his way of doing business and stay within the boundaries he sets them.

Having bought all his pubs in the same area, he has

now turned his sights outside the locality he knows so well. "My first six pubs were kept within a tight geographical area, which was considered a very hard place to succeed. But I have found it quite easy," he said. "Now I have to move away because there are only so many pubs you can have in Todmorden."

Paul Emery's tips

- Believe in yourself and be yourself. Stick to your convictions.
- Never say die – keep going even if things get bad.
- Be prepared to work hard – this is not a 9 to 5 business.
- Invest as much of your cash flow as possible in building up your business.
- Make every square centimetre of space generate revenue.
- Concentrate on achieving high standards and good customer care.
- Remember that happy customers spend money; unhappy ones don't.
- Have a strategy on how to develop your business.
- Keep pace with market trends and be prepared to change.

six

How to buy a hotel or guesthouse

*A*n introduction to the hotel sector. Do you have the right skills to be a hotelier? What kind of hotel or guesthouse do you want to buy? Is this the right hotel or guesthouse for you?

An introduction to the hotel sector

The hospitality industry – which includes hotels, guesthouses and restaurants – employs over 2 million people in 100,000 companies and supports over 200 trade associations.[1] (See page 124.) Although it is a mature and sophisticated industry, getting into it is relatively simple.

> **"Over the last 25 years hotel prices have maintained a close relationship with house prices and with the retail price index.'**

In some areas buying a hotel or guesthouse may not be much more costly than buying a family home. The market for private hotels is closely linked to the domestic housing market in two ways. First, as the value of domestic houses rises or falls, so does the amount of equity available to someone selling their house in order to buy a hotel. Secondly, a proportion of the value of a hotel is underpinned by the value of the "bricks and mortar". Over the last 25 years hotel prices have maintained a close relationship with house prices and with the retail price index.[2]

The price of a hotel, however, is also related to its profits and to its geographical location (the latter is of course also a feature of the domestic residential market). This means that, given relatively predictable hotel prices, there are great opportunities for those who are planning to sell a house in an expensive residential area to buy a larger hotel or guesthouse in another, less expensive area. A hotel can be a place to live, and so it is often a family home as well as a business that has the added advantage of generating income to support you and your family.

Do you have the right skills to be a hotelier?

It is important that your first research should be on yourself (see Chapter 2, pages 38–9). As you begin your search to buy a hotel or guesthouse, there are three areas you should attend to:

- *What skills do you need for the hospitality business?* You need to determine whether you are suited to owning and running a hotel. Are you prepared to work long, unsocial hours and to be available to your guests morning, noon and night?

- *What kind of hotel do you want to buy?* You must have knowledge of the hotel and guesthouse sector and know what kind of hotel you want to buy and run. You should build up a sense of what this industry is like, what drives its profits and what causes its losses.

- *Do you want to buy this particular hotel?* As you focus on the shortlist of hotels you are able to buy, there is a series of important questions you should ask about each one.

Related to these questions is market research into the hotels market, into local market conditions and demographic trends, and into hotel management. As you move forward with your ambition to buy, you can begin to piece together your Business Plan (see Chapter 3, pages 59–63). This plan will guide you as you run the business from day to day and enable you to predict its costs and income over time; it will also form an important part of the submission you might make to a mortgage lender.

> **"You should build up a sense of what this industry is like, what drives its profits and what causes its losses."**

The most important skill in the hospitality business is to like people, be prepared to look after them and put up with their invasion of your "home". You have to be emotionally intelligent, socially tolerant and personally easy going. As with any service business, you should have a clear idea about how you want to relate to your guests, what kind of customers you want to attract, and how you will develop personally along with the business.

The hospitality business is one of the easiest to enter without formal qualifications. However, formal qualifications are available through colleges and local training courses. Many of these can be acquired and worked for while running the business.[3] Search the Internet or look through the pages of the trade press, particularly *Caterer & Hotelkeeper*, for information on courses, menus, recipes, drinks, pricing, suppliers and equipment. It is also a good idea to spend time visiting other establishments for ideas. Develop your thinking and planning skills by reading widely and thinking seriously about the hotel industry.

> "Decide in advance what level of commitment... If you are a husband-and-wife team, will one of you keep your job or will you both work in the business?"

Decide in advance what level of commitment you are prepared to make. If you are a husband-and-wife team, will one of you keep your job or will you both work in the business? Do you want to have a bar? If you have a bar, you will increase your income, but are you prepared to spend time behind the bar pouring drinks? Do you want to provide bed-and-breakfast facilities only or will you also serve dinner? You may be good at dinner parties, but will you be able to deal with 30 people for dinner and as many again at breakfast? If not, you will have to consider taking on staff. Do you intend to invest in training?

What kind of hotel or guesthouse do you want to buy?

There are many different kinds of hotel and guesthouse and distinctions are not hard and fast. There are various ways of classifying hotels and types of hotel business. One is the Star-rating, which is determined by the type and extent of facilities on offer. Another is by the market segmentation of the hotel, as follows:

- Deluxe hotels.
- City hotels.
- Country house hotels.
- Corporate/conference hotels.
- Budget/lodge hotels.
- Townhouse/boutique hotels.
- Small proprietor-run hotels.

Hotels can also be ranked by the number of rooms or by their tariff. Generally speaking, independent hotels and guesthouses fall into a number of broad categories:

- *Guesthouses* – these tend to be smaller than hotels; they may not have a licensed bar, they will probably not have the kitchen facilities of a hotel, and they will probably not have facilities for functions, conferences and other events. Businesses of fewer than 10 to 12 rooms tend to be classed as guesthouses (unless they generate significant food and bev-erage turnover), whilst those with 10 to 20 rooms are viewed as small hotels, and those with 20 to 50 rooms as medium-sized hotels. It is sometimes possible to buy a large guesthouse and to convert or develop it into a hotel.

  > "It is sometimes possible to buy a large guesthouse and to convert or develop it into a hotel."

- *Coastal hotels or guesthouses* – these depend on holiday business and are therefore seasonal businesses. They tend to be smaller and family run. They are sometimes operated for part of the year only.

- *Country house hotels* – these are essentially leisure-based, offering high standards of accommodation, food and services. These are often in, or close to, prime tourist areas and offer a "home away from home". They quite often have leisure facilities such as a swimming pool, spa or gym.
- *Commercial or business hotels* – these are often on the outskirts of towns and cities that are well served by road and rail. Therefore, they attract business in the conference and corporate sectors, as well as leisure custom.
- *Hybrid hotels* – these derive their business from a mixture of seasonal trade, business clients, passing trade and all-year-round tourism. Generally, these hotels enjoy prime locations and, because of this, appeal to several types of clientele.
- *Boutique hotels or townhouse hotels* – these are a relatively new concept. Typically located in town or city centres, they are luxuriously furnished and/or design orientated. They generally occupy character buildings and their emphasis is on providing an extremely high quality of product and service at a rate that competes with larger mid-market or 4-Star hotels.
- *Budget hotels* – these are normally part of, or affiliated to, a chain and offer basic accommodation and limited service. They are usually modern and purpose-built.
- *Central London hotels* – these are often bought for medium- to long-term capital gain as much as for their capacity to produce revenue. This is a fairly specialist market where even a modest guesthouse can be priced at well over £1 million, and a medium-sized hotel at around £5 million. If you want to buy into this market you may be competing against overseas-based investors, many of whom are simply looking for a home for their money for a few years. Corporate operators, too, are often look-

ing for a flagship hotel in London. Initial return on investment can be considerably lower in London than in the regions because, traditionally, demand for hotels in London has been high, sites in short supply and building costs expensive.

These categories are by no means fixed; any category can have any number of bedrooms. In essence, any hotel or guesthouse could alter according to the kind of business it attracts.

As the market becomes more sophisticated, hotels must adapt to meet new demands. It is important that you keep up with trends and fashions in the industry. Perhaps the best ways to stay on top of the hotel market are to read widely, travel as much as you can, subscribe to the trade press and visit web sites. As you read statistics about the hotel market and consult indexes relating to the economic climate, always remember to take the long view. Never trust a single month's figures and be wary of seasonal adjustment.[4] It is often better to trust your own sense of the market, especially if you are already a hotel owner or have experience in running a hotel. Many factors can affect the hotels market. These might include the following:

> *"Perhaps the best ways to stay on top of the hotel market are to read widely, travel as much as you can, subscribe to the trade press and visit web sites."*

- Location.
- Design.
- Facilities.
- Fashion.
- Weather and holiday bookings.
- Transport costs and trends.
- Business cycles, which are an alchemical mix of interest rates, confidence, global currency

movements and local consumer borrowing – for example a strong pound discouraging overseas visitors.

- Interest rates.
- Availability of credit.
- Levels of public and private saving.
- Inflation.
- Business rates.
- Seasonal variations.
- Unforeseen and unpredictable events such as environmental crises – for example the foot-and-mouth outbreak and terrorist attacks in 2001.

Is this the right hotel or guesthouse for you?

First, after deciding whether you are suited to the hospitality business, you should have a clear idea about the type of hotel or guesthouse that you want to buy and the services you want to offer. Your background reading of the trade press and your contacts with business agents should have given you valuable information about the market, both nationally and regionally. Historical market information is important because you need to know how much prices might fluctuate and how much profits might vary given a variety of market conditions. These include high or low interest rates, high or low commodity and raw materials prices, and high or low inflation. Alongside this information you should be deciding how much money you can put into the business and, based on professional estimates, how much money you can expect to get out of it.

> *"Historical market information is important because you need to know how much prices might fluctuate and how much profits might vary..."*

Even though you may not know which hotel you will eventually buy and run, it is a great help at this stage to have a timetable to work to. Set yourself a target based on when you will complete your purchase. During this time you should have accumulated a great deal of knowledge about the kind of hotel you want to buy, how much you plan to spend and where you plan to be.

From business agents' lists, business property pages, web sites and other forms of advertising, you can draw up a shortlist of hotels that you want to look at. There are three fixed elements to any hotel or guesthouse: the *location*, the *buildings* and the *tenure* (see Appendix 2, pages 211–17).

Location

Consider the kind of location carefully. Do you want to be on the coast, where hotels are likely to rely on tourist trade and therefore be seasonal businesses; or in a town or city which is likely to attract both business and tourist trade all year round? If you are in a tourist area, it is likely that you will have to work extremely hard during the high season, and have little or no income out of season. The whereabouts and state of your competition is important here. If you are not already an experienced hotelier or guest-

> **"Consider the kind of location carefully. Do you want to be on the coast... or in a town or city..."**

house operator, think carefully about whether you should buy a hotel or guesthouse in a highly competitive area, such as the centre of a major city, where there are already many experienced operators. However, the advantage of competitive areas is that because they are popular with visitors, hoteliers will usually enjoy a high level of trade. Wherever you are looking to buy, investigate local competitors and assess the threats they pose.

Businesses that rely on tourists may well generate the same annual turnover as comparable hotels and guesthouses that have a mix of tourist and commercial clients throughout the rest of the year. However, tourist-based businesses will have their turnover concentrated in certain months of the year. Meanwhile, the bank loan and other overheads have to be paid throughout the year. A specialist business mortgage lender who knows the hotel market may be able to arrange seasonal repayment plans to accommodate lack of income in the low season. If the business you choose to buy is seasonal, take into account that your lender may provide only a partial loan of 60–65%, expecting you to invest the remainder.

All these factors will enable you to decide what price bracket you can afford to look in.

Buildings

When you have refined your search and chosen a hotel or guesthouse to buy, before you make an offer you should have a full survey and valuation undertaken (see Appendix 3). In particular, you should take an interest in the lease terms or freehold conditions. A survey will assess the physical condition of the accommodation, and you should pay particular attention to the owner's quarters and to the state of the public rooms and bedrooms.

The main features to be aware of are:

- *Owner's accommodation* – the hotel will probably be your family home, so it is important that you have the facilities you need, and that your family will be comfortable there. Just as you would take advice when buying a house, so you should here.
- *Business accommodation* – ask yourself some basic questions. Is the property in good condition and has it been regularly repaired and renovated? Does it have en suite bathrooms (these are important to guests these days)? Do all the public rooms and bedrooms meet fire and health and safety regulations?
- *Other facilities* – does the hotel have function/conference rooms; leisure facilities such as an indoor swimming pool, gym or games room; a restaurant; kitchens that are well equipped and well

maintained; staff accommodation which may be used for resident staff or converted to extra bedrooms to let?

Accounts/profitability

Ideally, the owner of the business you are proposing to buy will be able to provide you with both up-to-date and historical accounts (see Chapter 1, pages 27–35). Be wary of hotels that can't do this. You need to know how the business is trading now and how it has traded in the past, so it is useful to be able to see three years' accounts. Look carefully at the current cash flow and attach value to those businesses that can show you positive trading records for several years of operation. Examine the accounts and ask yourself questions such as: What are the current profit margins and are they too low or abnormally high? Are costs under control? Are wages excessive?

If full accounts are not available, there may be very good reasons for this. Always check these reasons thoroughly and, if necessary, brief your valuer to make checks on the hotel's viability.

> *"Ideally, the owner of the business you are proposing to buy will be able to provide you with both up-to-date and historical accounts."*

From the Profit and Loss Accounts and Balance Sheets you will be able to project the likely level of profit you will be able to achieve from the business, accepting that the existing owner's finance, depreciation and other non-operating costs may be different to yours. You might also have different requirements for staffing depending on how you intend running the business.

The level of profit from a guesthouse or small hotel can be high especially, for example, in the south east. An owner could expect a general turnover of between £50,000 and £100,000, with profits as high as 50%. Small central London hotels with, say, 10 bedrooms can have turnovers as high as £200,000, of which approximately 50% is likely to be profit. The typical turnover of a small guesthouse is £20,000 to £40,000.

As you look over the agent's details for the hotel or guesthouse you wish to buy, and as you question the business agents selling the business, you should ask the seller and/or the business agent questions such as:

- What kind of hotel is this?
- Where do its profits come from?
- How many rooms does the hotel have, and when are they occupied?
- What is the average occupancy rate? (See "Key ratios" at the end of this chapter.) You can find out average occupancy rates in your local area and nationally from your local and national tourist board, and by reading the trade press or accessing their web sites. How do this hotel's occupancy rates compare with those of its competitors?
- What is the average room rate? (See "Key ratios".)
- What is the revenue per available room? (See "Key ratios".)
- What might improve this hotel?
- Are there any local businesses to which the hotel could offer a service?
- Is there space to expand?
- What are the demographics of its customers? Where do they come from? What age are they? How much do they spend? How long do they stay?
- Could the turnover be increased through different sales or different customers, or by offering an improved service or new facilities?
- What is the competition within 30 minutes' or an hour's drive?
- Is this a trendy hotel that may go out of fashion in the future?
- Where do the profits come from predominantly – are they from upmarket or downmarket sources?

- What makes this hotel different? What are its Unique Selling Propositions (USPs)?
- Does its reputation depend on one chef, manager or owner?
- Does it do outside catering for parties, weddings, conferences and so on?
- Where can you add value? Examples are an extension, a new restaurant, different menus, a new head chef, additional facilities, refurbishment, improved marketing.
- Are there any long-stay guests? If so, what services do they require?

Once you have seen the business several times, and at different times of day, and you have had a chance to look over the accounts, you can begin to ask more detailed questions that relate to the way the present owners run the business and why they are selling:

> *"A busy, successful hotel takes energy and ideas to manage, and a deserted, unsuccessful hotel will take as much energy and money to change."*

- Why is this hotel on the market?
- How long has this owner been here?
- Has this owner done all they can with the hotel?
- Is the owner always tied up working in the bar or kitchen?
- Will any key staff leave when the current owner departs and, if so, how will this damage the business?

These are important questions, simply because you need to look at the life of the business very carefully before you commit yourself to it. A busy, successful hotel takes energy and ideas to manage, and a deserted, unsuccessful hotel will take as much energy and money to change.

Try to talk to the owners about their approach to the hotel and about what they have tried to do over the last few years – what has worked and what has failed, and why.

Local knowledge is a vital part of your research. The seller's agent should be able to help you with this. If the hotel has a bar or restaurant, remember that your competitors are not necessarily just other hotels, but also pubs, bars, cafés, restaurants and tourist centres.

You should know *who your customers are* and why and when they come to your hotel; and *who your potential customers are* and why and when they might come to your hotel. Then you can match your existing and potential customers with the facilities you have or plan to have.

> **"You should also establish contact with your local tourist board, which can help generate business for you as well as giving you advice on marketing."**

Look objectively at the facilities already in the hotel and also at the facilities you might want to add – a garden area, conservatory, or function room, for example – and then see if your competitors are offering anything similar. Try to offer something that no one else has.

Once you have identified what you have to offer, you can publicise and market the business by talking to journalists, getting into directories and listings and publicising yourself in order to promote your business. You should also establish contact with your local tourist board, which can help generate business for you as well as giving you advice on marketing.

Finally, you cannot ignore the Internet. Although relatively few bookings presently come over the net, it is a great medium for publicising your hotel and its facilities; and the potential for business in the future is substantial.[5]

Key ratios

- *Occupancy rate* – this is the number of rooms let as a percentage of the number of rooms available, over any given period.

- *Average room rate* – this is the average price achieved per bedroom let. These figures are also available from the sources mentioned on page 120. You need to ask if the average room rate could be increased to improve profit levels while staying competitive in your local market.

- *Revenue per available room* – this ratio recognises that not all rooms are available for letting all the time; some may be undergoing refurbishment or necessary maintenance. The higher the revenue generated per available room, the more profitable the hotel is likely to be. Check the hotel's figures against local and national levels from the sources listed on page 120.

> **"The profit generated can vary dramatically, depending on many factors – from the customer mix to the geographical location of the hotel."**

- *Ratio of net profit to turnover* – this shows at what rate every pound of turnover is converted into bottom-line profit. The profit generated can vary dramatically, depending on many factors – from the customer mix to the geographical location of the hotel. A hotel with more extensive food and beverage facilities will require more staff and have higher food/drink costs. In such a case, net profit to turnover might be 25%. On the other hand, a limited-service budget hotel where income is driven by the letting of bedrooms could generate 45% net profit to turnover.

- *Ratio of staff costs to turnover* – as a general rule, this can range from 20% in a hotel where relatively few staff are required to as high as 35% in a country house or 5-Star hotel where a high level of service is expected by guests. Make sure you know what type of hotel you are proposing to buy and whether the staff costs are in line with the kind of business operated.

Top tips

- Offer and give excellent service; always improve your quality.
- Network locally with other hoteliers and the local hotel association.
- Get marketing advice from the British Hospitality Association.
- Contact local companies who may need to accommodate employees, run conferences or seminars and entertain guests at lunch.
- Produce good-quality brochures, fliers and promotional material.
- Hire, train and retain good, trustworthy staff.
- Spend on upkeep and plan an on-going programme of refurbishment. Remember that external appearance is vital for passing trade.

Notes

1. *Caterer & Hotelkeeper*, 25 May 2000.
2. Christie & Co price indices, 1975–2001.
3. The British Institute of Innkeeping, British Hospitality Association, Hospitality Training Foundation and the Hotel & Catering International Management Association are all useful sources of information about training.
4. The highest grossing month in the South West is September, not entirely because of good weather, but also because of the surge in empty-nesters and semi-retired visitors who are bigger spenders than young families.
5. *The Caterer & Hotelkeeper Guide to the Internet* by David Grant and Peter McBride is an excellent source of information about how to use the Internet to improve your hospitality business.

hotels – a case study
Nigel Messenger: The Downfield Hotel, Stroud

Nigel Messenger had strict criteria when he set out to buy his own hotel: a spacious property with a big lounge, lots of storage space and enough car parking spaces; and a business that could trade 365 days of the year with both commercial and tourist guests. It therefore had to be on a main road close to tourist sites, and to have sufficient cash flow to repay a fairly sizeable loan. There also had to be the potential for improvement and expansion. That was his brief to his business agent. Initially he and his wife were looking for a 12-bedroom property but, when they found the 21-bedroom Downfield Hotel in Stroud, they changed their minds. They realised they would both have to work in this larger business.

Nigel had been Managing Director of Securicor Hotels, and he knew that there was a difference between his former role and his new one. "Managers are concerned with profit and owners are concerned with cash flow," he said. "Cash flow is everything. I'm into electronic banking and I check every day to make sure we are solvent."

When he was looking for a hotel, he was able to judge quickly if a business was viable by working out its profits and then adding in the repayment of finance. If the figures stacked up, the property was worth further investigation. He is astounded at how little research many prospective buyers do before acquiring their business: "We booked into a local hotel and talked to the manager and the staff to find out about other hotels in the area. Without their advice, we would have been in trouble. It is vital to get behind the facts you have been given."

> *"What drove both of us was the absolute excitement of being independent and throwing off the shackles of our lives being controlled by someone else."*

Looking back on his first week at the helm, he recalls it as "absolutely, utterly dreadful". The credit card machine didn't work and he didn't know how to swipe cards anyway. "I had never cleaned beer pipes before, didn't know how to operate a switchboard or even the computers and fax – everything was a steep learning process. Plus, everyone wants you to sign new contracts, and on top of everything, we were also moving our home, which is fraught enough," he said.

"I think we both got four hours' sleep a night in that first week. But I've never once wondered if I did the right thing. What drove both of us was the absolute excitement of being independent and throwing off the shackles of our lives being controlled by someone else. We had our own home, our own hotel, our own customers and we could make our own decisions."

Despite a tough first week, Nigel Messenger believes things could have been worse without the help of the previous owners, who (most irregularly) let the

Messengers move in before the contract was signed and who helped out at the hotel for a couple of days. "We didn't haggle over the price which we thought was very reasonable, so in return the previous owners were very helpful. If we had taken a different attitude, they might not have been so co-operative," he says. "I had worked in the hotel sector for 30 years, but I have learned more in the last 2 years than I had learned in the previous 30."

Nigel Messenger's tips

- Don't take anything you are told at face value – research the facts.
- Talk to local hoteliers – they will tell you if you are about to buy a turkey.
- However much you think your start-up costs will be, double them. Suppliers want money up front when you are a new customer.
- Be prepared to invest more of your savings if you hit a quiet patch.
- Keep an eagle eye on your cash flow at all times.
- Look very hard at the contract and at the detail of what is included in the sale and what is not.
- Look very carefully at the accounts; if the present owners are doing the work of seven people, you will have to employ more staff and, as a result, your costs will be higher than theirs.
- Get the former owners on your side; you will need their help.
- Don't rush into doing anything in the business or making snap judgements. It takes time to understand why things are done in a certain way.

seven

How to buy a restaurant

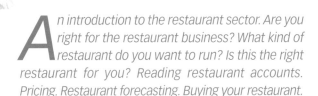

*A*n introduction to the restaurant sector. Are you right for the restaurant business? What kind of restaurant do you want to run? Is this the right restaurant for you? Reading restaurant accounts. Pricing. Restaurant forecasting. Buying your restaurant.

An introduction to the restaurant sector

It is hard to quantify accurately the size of the restaurant market in the UK, but the number of restaurants – not including cafés that serve food – is estimated to be around 25,000 to 26,000, serving 660 million meals in a year and accounting for nearly 20% of all UK food sales.[1] (See page 144.) Of those, over 18,000 are independents, owned by people who have bought and now run their own restaurant. The remainder are group-owned restaurants. From these figures it is clear that the restaurant sector is large and diverse. Its turnover amounts to several billions, and it is clear that independent business people play a vital role in its health and prosperity.

In buying a restaurant, the same fundamentals apply as in buying any business. First, you must decide if you are temperamentally suited to the restaurant business; next you must decide on the type of restaurant you wish to buy and run; and finally you must set about searching for and buying your restaurant.

> *"You should be thinking about the type of restaurant you want to run and the services you want to offer."*

As you are searching for the restaurant you want to buy, you should be piecing together elements of your Business Plan. Of course, you cannot know the exact details at this point, but you should be thinking about the type of restaurant you want to run and the services you want to offer. You should also be thinking about how much money you can put into the business and about how much money you expect to get out of it. Almost without exception, those restaurants that fail do so either because their owners do not manage their cash flow or because they have borrowed too much money in the first instance. Both situations can be avoided by making careful plans and following good advice early on.

It will help to make a plan of action as you start out to buy a restaurant. It makes sense to treat this as a new business – after all, it is new to you – and to take the same precautions as you would if you were starting from scratch. The plan is essential. It allows you to set targets, to make sense of all your research into the area, and to give yourself a clear picture of where you are in your search. You should begin this plan by drawing up a timetable.

Of course, there is a distinction between buying an existing restaurant and starting your own restaurant. Starting a restaurant from scratch is the harder of the two options; buying an existing one can be relatively straightforward. It will be much easier to borrow money in order to finance a business that is continuing than to finance one that is starting up.

Bear in mind that if you decide, for example, to buy a restaurant serving Italian food and want to change it immediately into one serving Indian food, you would lose the continuity – and possibly your existing customers – which is so important in running a business. Nonetheless, it is very common for people to buy one type of restaurant and change it into another.

In all the instances outlined, whether or not you are experienced in the restaurant business, you need to have an adequate plan which includes a Business Plan and a Financial Plan (see Chapter 3).

Are you right for the restaurant business?

At this point you must be honest with yourself (see Chapter 2). If you love being in charge, taking risks, assuming responsibility, working hard and unsocial hours; if you have stamina, vision, persistence and courage, and like dealing with customers – then you are probably suited to running your own restaurant. If you prefer someone else to make your decisions or feel you may lack the will to struggle through the difficult periods that are common in any business, you should go and work with or for someone else in the restaurant business for a while before deciding to go into business on your own.

> *"If you have stamina, vision, persistence and courage, and like dealing with customers – then you are probably suited to running your own restaurant."*

Owning and running a restaurant requires no professional qualifications, and involves no commuting if you live on the premises. The restaurant business calls for qualities of character, stamina, risk-taking, creativity and sound business sense. You have to be physically fit to handle a busy night in a restaurant, and temperamentally strong to handle a slow night or the odd difficult customer.

A good restaurateur should be calm and tolerant of all ranges of behaviour – from the fractious toddler with indulgent parents through to the rude client who books, and thinks nothing of arriving an hour late. It helps to have a quick mind, a ready smile, and a temperament that does not allow small setbacks to discourage or depress you. If you have these qualities in some measure, and if you enjoy people, you are likely to prosper in the restaurant business.

The restaurant is essentially a two-function business: one in the kitchen dealing with the food, and the other at the front of house dealing with the customers. These call for two distinct sets of skills and, although the picture of the genius chef emerging only to berate customers for adding salt and pepper to their creations is a popular one in the media, it is not realistic in practice. Neither is the notion of the front-of-house manager suddenly whipping up an amazing dish in the kitchen. The skills for the daily operation of a restaurant need to be developed alongside the skills needed to run a business. If this restaurant is your first business, you need to concentrate on learning how to handle money, goods, customers, authorities, staff and family.

As you think about your personal suitability for the catering business, it is worth reviewing what catering experience you have. It is highly advisable to have some direct knowledge of the catering trade; if you lack this, get it by working for someone else for a few months. This will have various benefits:

- You will gain some inside knowledge of what it is like to work in the kitchen and to wait at tables.
- You will find out what it is like to be a member of staff.
- Your experience and knowledge should mean that it is more likely that your staff – when you have them – will respect your decisions and not try to take advantage of you.
- You will learn the jargon, the tricks of the trade, and you will be paid while you learn.

Apart from work experience, there are plenty of training courses available to you. Go on courses to improve your cooking and business management skills. Build up a fund of ideas – keep a record of good ideas (and bad ones too) gained from every restaurant you go into. Use a notebook to write down useful things you read, hear, think or want to know. Get your ideas from your own experience, your friends and your read-

> *"Build up a fund of ideas – keep a record of good ideas (and bad ones too) gained from every restaurant you go into."*

ing; go to courses and open days; glean ideas from competitors, especially from the type of restaurant you plan to run. Talk to restaurateurs past and present, read the professional press – particularly the *Caterer & Hotel-keeper*, the Restaurant Association's *Dine Out* magazine, *Restaurant Business* and *Theme* – and subscribe to news groups and bulletin boards on the Internet to learn and exchange information about the business. There is a vast array of statistical and market information in the trade media (eg *Caterer & Hotelkeeper* and its web site www.caterer.com). These encompass annual surveys, research, news, trends and current prices of everything from fresh produce to kitchen and restaurant equipment.

One of the best places to start looking for information about the UK restaurant industry is the Restaurant Association.[2] It deals with matters of regulation and licensing, staffing and employment relations, education and training, service charges, food safety and the range of legislation and other issues that will affect how you run your restaurant. It also works with around 50 approved Patron Suppliers, who offer products and services to full members, often at discounted rates. These services range from discounts on credit and debit card processing rates and business insurance to free legal and health and hygiene help-lines. Good business agents who sell restaurants, pubs, and hotels, both in your area and nationally, can also be important allies. They will be a primary source of ideas and information.

> "Entering the restaurant business may be a good way to build up your wealth, but it will not happen immediately."

Entering the restaurant business may be a good way to build up your wealth, but it will not happen immediately. Neither will you be able to live off the business for probably the first 6 to 12 months. There are a number of fixed costs which have to be met whether or not people are eating in your restaurant: examples are mortgage payments, staff wages and salaries, insurance, business rates and rent, repairs, heat, light, telephone, marketing, advertising and so on. In the early stages, these costs will probably exceed the income and this must be planned for.

What kind of restaurant do you want to run?

The restaurant market is developing and expanding to embrace new concepts and new styles. Pubs, clubs, hotels, cafés, museums, railway stations, department stores, health clubs and community centres are all offering food. Generally, however, there are five kinds of restaurant:

- *Fast-food take-aways* – these are essentially production lines where the food is provided by specialist food suppliers. They are often managed or franchised and invariably corporate owned; décor, menus, staff uniforms, marketing and company culture all come from head office, so there is little scope for entrepreneurs other than as investors in the business.

- *Snack bars, tea shops, coffee shops and cafés* – in essence, there are two markets here: private cafés and corporate coffee shops. In the 1990s the latter emerged as coffee and tea specialists and started to serve hot beverages on the high street; this trend is continuing with soup, juice and bagels. These are often corporate owned but are sometimes owned and run by entrepreneurial independents.

- *Ethnic or speciality restaurants* – the customers here are those who wish to eat specific kinds of food. The main types of ethnic food in the UK are various types of European (French, Italian etc), Indian and Chinese; outlets selling these make up over a third of all restaurants.[3] They are invariably owned and run by independents rather than corporates.

- *Bistros and cafés* – the competition here is with the established chains, pubs, hotels and theme restaurants. Here, restaurant design is important as well as the kind of food served since customers eating in this type of establishment are looking for a dining "experience". These are often chains of restaurants owned by corporates, but many are operated by independents and there is great scope for the independent owner.

- *Fine-dining restaurants* – the customers here usually spend more, but the restaurant costs much more to run, staff, refurbish, advertise and maintain than any other type of restaurant business. By definition, there are fewer potential customers but they are high spenders. These tend to be owned by independents, often chefs; some are Michelin rated or are seeking culinary accolades.

> "Restaurants and cafés are in constant flux as new fashions and new technologies emerge. No two businesses are the same..."

These five broad types will, in turn, be influenced by the location of the restaurant: city, suburban or rural. Restaurants and cafés are in constant flux as new fashions and new technologies emerge. No two businesses are the same and you should try to see each on its own terms. For example, a café business in Manchester may be a better business proposition than a select gourmet restaurant in rural Oxfordshire.

Is this the right restaurant for you?

Once you have decided on what kind of place you want to own and run, you then have to set about looking for one. This is far from simple because there are so many variables to consider. You will probably be searching not only by restaurant type, but also by geographical location and price range. The trade press and business agents are the best places to start in order to get a sense of the market. Your decision may be shaped by the range of restaurants available in the area in which you wish to buy; or it may be determined by a strong business idea you have. Either way, when you are looking at a prospective restaurant, the answer to whether it is right for you depends on a number of factors:

- Is this a good location for this type of restaurant?
- Is it leasehold or freehold?
- Is the building in good condition and can it be extended?
- Who are the current and target customers and where do they come from?
- What style of restaurant and cuisine do you want to offer?
- What local conditions apply, and on what days?
- Where can you add value – for example extend the size of the restaurant, change its style, expand and change the menus, refurbish, improve the marketing, organise special events?
- Where is the competition and what are they doing?
- What is the most popular local restaurant and why?
- What makes this restaurant distinctive?
- How can this business balance what is popular with what is different?
- What is the image of this restaurant? Can you change it? Do you need to change it?

The location is one of the fixed points you must deal with when you think about buying a restaurant. Once you have bought, you are committed to that location and cannot change it. Make sure you have a sense of

> *"...find out if there are local offices/businesses or residential blocks of flats that could provide you with customers."*

how the location affects the business. For example, try counting passers-by at different times of the day; and find out if there are local offices/businesses or residential blocks of flats that could provide you with customers.

As you begin your search, you will encounter restaurants for sale under several different arrangements. The most common of these are leasehold, freehold, franchise (see Appendix 2) and concession.

A *concession* is the right to do business as a caterer at various events and locations – such as race meetings, festivals, exhibitions or shows, shopping centres, railway stations and airports. Usually, the holder of the concession sets up for a few days or a week at the client's venue – sometimes in a temporary setting like a marquee.

It is likely that a *franchise* will be cheaper to buy and to run than a restaurant you own yourself, but you will have little scope for self-expression in this type of business.

Whatever the type of restaurant and whatever its location, it is important to visit as a client at various times of the day. Ideally, you should also try to eat in your prospective restaurant at specific times during the year. By visiting the restaurant at various times – or by asking your friends to do so – you will gain a clearer sense of what you might add to the business (breakfast or brunch, theme nights, promotions and so on). If the restaurant is listed in any guidebooks, read all the reviews, and look for any local press write-ups about it.

> "Whatever the type of restaurant and whatever its location, it is important to visit as a client at various times of the day."

Reading restaurant accounts

You can use your analysis of a restaurant's accounts as part of the information in your Financial Plan. By far the most important factor is cash flow, and within that the most important thing is making accurate projections of expenses rather than sales or demand. In the UK the Restaurant Association[4] is a useful source of information while, for those with an eye on US comparisons, the

National Restaurant Association produces sample operating statistics and figures which are typical for a range of American restaurants from fast-food outlets to top-of-the-market, full-service establishments.[5]

It should be possible to tell from the accounts the profits that derive from the sale of wine and other alcoholic drinks, and those that derive from food. You may decide that you can alter the ratio between the two and this in itself may alter your profits. Remember that different people keep accounts in very different ways, and that a profit for one person may not be a profit for another. Likewise, a loss for one business owner may well translate into a profit for another simply because people's circumstances are different.

> *"Price alone will not bring customers into a restaurant; but an astute combination of this, the right product, service and image will."*

Pricing

One of the key factors you must consider before you buy is the type of business that your prospective restaurant attracts. This depends not only on its location and on the type of food offered, but on the prices it charges, the number of seats it has and, most important, the number of covers (or meals) it serves. In principle, the more covers you serve, the higher the potential profits. Price alone will not bring customers into a restaurant; but an astute combination of this, the right product, service and image will. There may be scope for you to change the business and offer something different, more profitably.

There are four basic approaches to pricing food and drink in restaurants:

- *Full-cost pricing* – this takes account of costs, and incorporates a profit margin for the restaurant. This is stable but expensive for the customers.
- *Specific mark-ups* – this is a flexible way of pricing

what you sell, and allows the business to react both to demand from customers and to supply from suppliers. This is often the best way to sell seasonal dishes.

- *Gross margin pricing* – this takes account of advertising and marketing costs and basic expenses.
- *The market rate* – charge whatever competitors are charging (or slightly less) and react to prices as they move.

Each pricing policy should weigh price with quality, service, ambience, convenience, value, health and safety and so on. The best people to advise about the type of pricing structure in force in restaurants are the restaurateurs themselves. By asking them how menu prices are calculated you should gain a clear idea of how best to structure your own pricing. If there seems to be an opportunity for greater profit or greater savings, make a note of it and follow it up after you have bought the restaurant. Whatever you do, make sure you can cover your fixed business expenses and still have a reasonable profit after any tax you have to pay.

> *"Whatever you do, make sure you can cover your fixed business expenses and still have a reasonable profit after any tax you have to pay."*

Restaurant forecasting

If you are buying an existing restaurant, forecasting is relatively easy since you will have some sense of the historical figures. If you have examined these with an accountant or business agent skilled and experienced in this area of business, you will have quite dependable figures. On the basis of monthly cash flows and receipts for the past few months of trading, you should be able to produce a figure for the total sales and also have some idea of the average amount people spend (known as "the spend") and the number of meals sold. These figures will vary by month, week, day and time of day, so an average is only a rough guide. Nonetheless, it is useful for forecasting not only cash flow but also profit and loss.

When you come to predict your expenses, you should have historical data regarding the costs, no matter who the owner of the business is. These include wages, utilities, rates and so on. It might be wise to produce three forecasts for the business when under your ownership – one for low sales and high expenses, one for average sales and average expenses, and one for high sales and low expenses.

Be pessimistic, or at least conservative; it is easier to spend than to save, easier to incur more expenses and harder to create more sales. Cash comes to you more slowly and expenses more quickly than you might imagine.

Consider using a software package specially designed for cash flow predictions in the restaurant business and make sure you fill in your monthly outgoings (eg mortgage, wages, rentals, banking and credit-handling costs) and your occasional outgoings (eg utilities, insurance, legal bills, taxes). Then calculate your monthly income in the form of cash sales, including sales that you can treat as cash such as debit card and credit card payments.

> *"Be pessimistic, or at least conservative; it is easier to spend than to save, easier to incur more expenses and harder to create more sales."*

Look over your cash flow for the first year you plan to be in business. It helps to calculate a cumulative cash flow, so that you can see at a glance at what point in the year you might need extra money to cover the outgoings before you receive the income to cover them.

Buying your restaurant

Once you have completed your research on yourself, on the type of restaurant, on the location, and on the specific business you want to buy, you have only to finish the actual purchase. Before you do that, learn what else you can. Although the agent acting for the seller is not representing you, they can be of great help in taking you through the process in such a way that everybody benefits. It is essential to have a Structural Survey and Valuation Report for the restaurant you want to buy (see Appendix 3).

The Valuation Report gives you the facts and figures and the Structural Survey any physical defects you might take on; it also provides you with a negotiating position when you come to make your offer. The restaurant accounts should show the trend of profit or loss over the previous three or four years; any restaurant reviews would also be helpful.

Ask the owner why the restaurant is for sale, and listen carefully to the answer. There may be a range of factors that affect the accounts that are particular to the present owner; examples are health, age and future plans for the business.

While it is impossible to change the site and situation of the restaurant premises, it may be possible to change many other of its characteristics. You can re-fit, re-furbish and then re-launch a restaurant to present a new style of cooking and décor, and, most important, to attract new customers. You are free to change anything you want on the menus.

But think twice about changing a winning formula; if the restaurant is successful when you buy it, you should do everything you can *not* to change it. That may involve analysing why the restaurant is successful in the first place and what is likely to alter when you take over.

Key ratios

- *Ratio of net profit to turnover* – this depends on the style of restaurant and the number of staff it has to employ. Take-away or buffet restaurants will have a considerably higher net profit margin – up to 35% –

because they employ fewer staff and have a faster through-put. They tend not to be sited in a prime location, so overheads are lower. Many ethnic restaurants also generate high net profits because they employ members of the owner's family. As a general rule, a casual diner will have a net profit-to-turnover ratio of 15–20% while a fine-dining restaurant's profit will be more like 10–15% because food costs and wastage will be much higher. In addition, the latter type of restaurant employs a higher ratio of staff per customer, so staff costs are also higher.

- *Ratio of staff costs to turnover* – in a fine-dining restaurant, staff costs should be no more than 30–35% of turnover; in a casual restaurant, no more than 25%; and in a take-away or fast-food operation, no more than 20%.

- *Number of covers or meals served in relation to the number of seats* – if a restaurant has 50 seats but serves only one customer per seat per evening, the maximum number of meals it can

> "Make sure you ask about the number of covers served and consider whether you will be able to increase this."

serve per evening is 50. If the restaurant serves two customers per seat per evening, it can double its turnover. Make sure you ask about the number of covers served and consider whether you will be able to increase this.

Top tips

- Assess things before you change them and be careful about spending too much.
- Hire, train and retain good, trustworthy staff.
- Join the Restaurant Association to benefit from the competitive prices offered by its 40–50 Patron Suppliers, all of which work closely with the asso-

ciation and offer products and services to members, often at discounted rates.

- Join your local restaurant association to benefit from its marketing efforts. Some of the larger associations can offer you better buying power.

- Forge links with tourist boards to benefit from cheaper advertising and any local marketing material/campaigns.

- Advertise locally and build up effective public relations to get your restaurant written about.

- Change the menu regularly.

- Extend your opening hours and be flexible.

Notes

1. Foodservice Intelligence figures, 2000; food sales were £4.046 billion; food purchases by restaurants were £1.8 billion.
2. See www.ragb.co.uk
3. Foodservice Intelligence figures, 2000.
4. See www.ragb.co.uk; similar information is available at www.caterer.com, the web site of *Caterer & Hotelkeeper*.
5. See www.restaurant.org

restaurants – a case study
Donald Malcolm: Sarah Janes coffee shop, Stirling

When Donald Malcolm retired from the Royal Navy, he decided to turn his back on marine engineering and buy a small coffee shop/snack bar in Stirling, Scotland. Buying Sarah Janes coffee shop was not an instant decision but the result of seven years' planning before he retired. His research involved walking around the town and looking at all the catering outlets to see where there were opportunities.

Before buying the business he looked at empty properties and assessed the cost of re-fitting them. The advantages of Sarah Janes were that the business had been trading for 25 years, was well established and was in the right location.

He remembers his first week in the business as "like hitting the ground running". Fortunately, the previous owner stayed on for another week to help him. "I shadowed her for the first week, which was very good of her as she didn't want to be paid," he said. "You think it must be easy making a cup of coffee, but there's a knack to putting steam through the milk. I also found it tough working with women after so long in the Navy. In all, it was a complete change in routine, but I knew it would be, so it wasn't much of a shock."

Initially, he had plenty of ideas about how he would like to change the business, including its name, but he soon realised the coffee shop had built up a good reputation over 25 years; there was no point in risking throwing that away. At first he thought he would change the brand of coffee, until he understood that Sarah Janes was selling the best coffee in town. Now he plans to use the sales and marketing skills he learned as part of the forces re-settlement package to publicise his business, putting established skills to new uses.

> *"At first he thought he would change the brand of coffee, until he understood that Sarah Janes was selling the best coffee in town."*

The only problem he faced was finding money to buy his business. "I thought banks were throwing money at people, but although I was putting up the money for half of the business, they still wanted the collateral of my house, life insurance policies etc," he recalled. "I went round all the banks and in the end I had to offer my house as collateral, plus an endowment policy."

Before buying Sarah Janes, he carefully read through the business's accounts. "You can read a lot about the business through the accounts. The previous owner had three outlets and a lot of the expenses were staff costs, which I was able to reduce as I could do the work myself," he said.

Donald Malcolm's tips

- Research the market before you start looking for a property.
- It costs much more to find new customers than it does to keep existing ones.
- Find out what your customers want, but remember the customer is not always right!
- Make all your customers feel special.
- Make sure your restaurant is clean and tidy and staff are friendly.
- Nothing should be too much trouble, no matter how busy you are.

eight

How to buy a retail business

An introduction to the retail sector. Do you have the right skills? What kind of retail business do you want to buy? Aspects of retail. Is this the right retail business for you? Freehold, leasehold or franchise?

An introduction to the retail sector

Retail is a £200 billion business that makes up 23% of the UK's Gross Domestic Product. It is a large, diverse and growing sector which provides goods and, increasingly, services to 24 million households. Each of those households spends an average of £144 each week in retail outlets; of that £144, the biggest single proportion (around £45, or 31%) is spent on food and non-alcoholic drinks.

The retail sector as a whole is growing at between 2% and 2.5% a year; and there are nearly 2.5 million retail workers in the UK, that is around one in nine of the UK workforce. Of course, many are employees, but a high proportion of the 321,000 retail outlets in the UK are owned and run by individuals and small companies.

> "... a high proportion of the 321,000 retail outlets in the UK are owned and run by individuals and small companies."

The sector is relatively easy and cheap to enter, with little specialist training required. With low financial entry levels, the profits on small retail businesses may be lower than some larger hospitality businesses that may require a bigger investment. However, retail is often a high-volume turnover business with lower margins, which can produce a good return on capital employed.

Food retail is a mature and developing market. It includes supermarket chains (eg Tesco, Sainsbury's), niche operators (eg Co-op, Budgens) and independent operators sometimes trading under buying groups (eg Londis, Spar). Few independents operate stores of more than 900 sq m; most run stores of 45–140 sq m. Stores appear on the market either because other independents are selling them or because a multiple store owner is changing the make-up of its business and selling stores that are not sufficiently profitable under management but which nonetheless would be profitable for an independent operator. The high volume of sales in the food, drink and convenience store sector means that although competition in some parts of the sector is fierce, there is always space for the independent operator.

> *"You need a clear understanding of how the business will produce profits and how it will support any borrowing costs you may have."*

When thinking of buying a retail business, the most important questions you need to address are the following:

- Do you have the right skills? Are you suited to owning and running a retail business?
- What kind of retail business do you want to buy? There is an increasing variety of specialist retail businesses emerging as suppliers, markets and demographics change constantly. Opportunities are there for the quick witted and the imaginative.
- What is the status and health of the specific retail business you are considering buying? You need a clear understanding of how the business will produce profits and how it will support any borrowing costs you may have.

Do you have the right skills?

There are many reasons why a person may choose to enter the retail sector as an independent owner–operator. There are great rewards and much satisfaction in owning and running a retail business or chain of retail businesses. A wide variety of people arrive at this point from many starting places and at various stages in life. Your success rests with you and on your personal abilities and energies.

Your own retail business should give you scope for using individual judgement and personal initiative, and it should give you access to, and contact with, a wide range of people.

Many first-time retailers are experienced in other forms of business and can bring skills from many working backgrounds. You might start by asking what you like doing and what you are good at:

- Do you enjoy serving others?
- Are you ambitious? If you want to build a chain of stores, you may be better off in areas of dense population, near customers in towns and cities. If your main impetus for change is a less pressured lifestyle, a rural location would perhaps be best.
- Do you understand how retail works? Sales, profit margins, costs, net profits and stock values are all important concepts. These are not difficult to master, but it is important that you do so.

Your personal leanings and those of your personal and/or business partner, if any, may well determine the kind of retail business you want to buy. If you have little or no experience in the retail market, you can easily gain some by working for someone else before you buy your own business. There are many training resources available – from colleges, small business groups, trade associations, industry training boards, local business organisations and development agencies. (See Appendix 5). Courses will not teach you what it is really like to run your own business, but they will give you a sense of the pains and pleasures of the new responsibilities you will be taking on. Two of the most important skills you can learn from a course in retailing are financial management and stock control.

What kind of retail business do you want to buy?

Look at any high street, market, shopping centre or village centre and you will see the widest possible variety of shops and retail businesses. There is also a huge range of variation between what is sold, when it is sold, and where it is sold. Add the impact of e-commerce and mail order, and the picture becomes even more interesting.

The best way to determine what retail business you want to go into is to look around, ask questions and read widely.[1] (See page 164.) Almost any kind of retail business can be taken over and run by someone with little experience and limited knowledge of the specific retail field (examples are stationers, kitchen and bathroom outlets, drapery shops, gift stores etc). However, specialist knowledge does help, especially if you will have to deal immediately with knowledgeable customers in areas such as computing or electrical retailing. As an initial purchase, it may be better to look at retail businesses that meet some basic needs for their customers; for example food, drink, money exchange and reading matter. The outlets for these are various permutations of convenience store, post office and newsagent.

> *"Almost any kind of retail business can be taken over and run by someone with little experience and limited knowledge of the specific retail field."*

Convenience/grocery store

There are nearly 36,000 stores of this kind in the UK.[2] The convenience store is much more profitable than the traditional grocery store, principally because it can offer an "emergency purchase" out of supermarket hours, close to customers' work, homes or commuting routes. Convenience stores offer a complementary service to the big supermarkets by trading longer hours for seven days a week, offering specific goods to suit local needs. You should match your trading hours as closely as possible to popular demand. Late night and weekend trading may be profitable in one area but not in another. The convenience store, which evolved in the 1970s, is in the midst of a period of rapid change which will see the c-store of the future being fresher, brighter and bigger. But as supermarket chains continue to search for new profits, and as retail space becomes scarcer and more costly, chains of supermarket-owned convenience stores – often in towns and cities and often open for long hours – are adding increased competition. However, many independent operators are able to meet this challenge by gathering together in buying groups to sell branded and own-label produce.

Newsagents and confectioners–tobacconists–newsagents (CTNs)

There are over 31,500 of these stores in the UK.[3] Stores of this kind tend to have long opening hours, especially those with deliveries and news rounds. Over-the-counter newsagent sales are the easiest to manage, but do not have the same guaranteed income that deliveries provide. Since 1990 news supplies have become more liberal, and newspapers can now be bought from a variety of retail outlets. Successful newsagents either specialise in terms of the service they offer (home deliveries) and in the papers and magazines available (eg foreign language titles), or diversify by bringing new goods and services into the store. A store may be small, but it should aim to be the strongest newsagent in the area.

> "Newsagents are attractive to potential purchasers for various reasons. They are small... and historically quite cheap, and they offer a good return on capital."

Newsagents are attractive to potential purchasers for various reasons. They are small (40–55 sq m) and historically quite cheap, and they offer a good return on capital. They also offer a relatively secure income – particularly businesses with news deliveries and stable sales – thereby allowing purchasers to work full-time in the business and earn money for a relatively low investment. There are good profits to be made in selling ancillary items like gifts, stationery and greetings cards – the kinds of things shoppers like to buy locally and in a small-scale environment. The location of a retail business of this kind is the key to its success.

Post offices

There are over 18,000 post offices (including sub-post offices) in the UK.[4] The sub-post office often operates alongside a retail business such as those described on the previous pages. It might be a commercial franchise, an independent franchise or – most commonly – an agency office. Sub-post offices in rural areas, despite the difficult phase in their development in the 1990s,[5] remain one of the cornerstones of rural communities, where they often operate as a village store. Special conditions apply. Sub-post offices offer a secure income and an assured flow of customers to support the retail side of the business; often complementary services such as computing, Internet, fax and photocopying can be profitable. Post Office Limited (POL) offers a range of products and services,[6] serving 28 million customers a week. This market changes constantly, partly because of market forces and partly because of government policy – for example, the Universal Bank will offer a range of products and services through post offices.

Off-licences and food stores

Alongside the types of store already mentioned, there are over 11,000 off-licences and 36,500 non-grocery food stores such as bakeries, delicatessens, wet fish shops, butchers and so on.

Hybrid businesses

These include post offices with card outlets or newsagents/convenience stores, and are increasingly popular. Many newsagents and convenience stores have National

Lottery terminals and this increases turnover and profit. Often the work schedules of a business can be complementary; for example, the bulk of a newsagent's work is often done before 9 am when the post office opens. Of course, in reality many stores are hybrid businesses.

> *"Many purchasers are looking to buy a way of life as well as a well-established business with its property in good repair."*

Lifestyle businesses

These are businesses, eg village stores or post offices, situated in attractive rural areas, particularly in small towns and villages. Many purchasers are looking to buy a way of life as well as a well-established business with its property in good repair (see Chapter 2, pages 41–4). In some cases they are prepared to travel hundreds of miles to view the right business.

Aspects of retail

One way of looking at businesses is to consider first the size of store you might want to buy. Small independent convenience stores, most often in a suburban location, tend to have between 45 and 140 sq m of retail or selling space; larger convenience stores run by corporate operators tend to have between 140 and 280 sq m of retail space. Retail space is expensive in the UK (around twice the cost of that in the EU),[7] so it must be made to work hard for the retailer. The industry norm for convenience store turnover is around £100 per square metre per week. Higher turnovers are possible in urban locations, trading 24 hours; these might achieve £300 per square metre.[8] Changing lifestyles and different working and eating habits have an effect on the appeal of major supermarkets and relatively small convenience stores.[9] As home delivery becomes more prominent (with e-commerce, mail order, direct supply of organic goods etc), small stores that offer the essential elements lacking in large supermarkets – namely human contact and personal service – may prosper.

Another way of thinking about the retail sector is to consider turnover. This, together with gross profit, is the most important figure to look at. A good CTN should have a turnover of between £5,000 and £10,000 plus per week; an off-licence should have a turnover of between £4,000 and £10,000 plus per week; an independent convenience store should have a turnover of between £4,000 and £15,000 plus per week; and a corporate convenience store should have a turnover of around £15,000 per week or more. The most important aspect of these figures is the comparative levels of gross profit derived. Be aware of items that are based on commission: lottery sales, parking permits, bus passes, stamps, dry cleaning and so on. The commission should be seen as income and should be recorded separately from other sales.

> *"Changing lifestyles and different working and eating habits have an effect on the appeal of major supermarkets and relatively small convenience stores."*

It is difficult to put exact gross profit margins on products because different stores have different pricing policies. However, here are some guide figures for gross profits you should look for:

- *Groceries* – 18 to 24%.
- *Confectionery* – 21 to 24%.
- *Newspapers and magazines* – 25%.
- *Off-licence* – 18 to 22%.
- *Household goods* – 25 to 30%.
- *Cards and stationery* – 40 to 50%.
- *Fruit and vegetables* – 30 to 35%.
- *Gifts* – 40 to 50%.
- *Tobacco* – 7 to 9%.

Higher-margin goods – such as cards, stationery and gifts – tend to be lower volume and require higher levels of stock. It is vital to think about the mix of sales when you are confronted with a set of figures for turnover and gross profits. Goods such as cut-price tobacco or alcohol will boost turnover without necessarily boosting profits. For these items the profit margin may be as low as 2–3%. This is often deliberately set at a low level in order to attract people into the shop and thereby increase "foot-fall".

Yet another way of thinking about the retail sector is the low cost of entry. Retail businesses are usually available as leasehold or freehold (see Appendix 2). A substantial element of the purchase price for most retail businesses will be goodwill, which is usually based on a multiple of the profitability of the business, depending on a number of variables such as location, local environment, the quality of the property and accommodation and trading hours. The stock is not normally part of the purchase price and is usually valued separately and purchased in addition at cost. Depending on the sector, this may be a significant part of the overall investment you will have to make in the business. For a food retailer or newsagent, the stock will probably be around three weeks' turnover, while the figure for cards and stationery will probably be around ten weeks.

> "It is vital to think about the mix of sales when you are confronted with a set of figures for turnover and gross profits."

Is this the right retail business for you?

The value of any retail business unit depends on many things, including the potential to extend the sales area and to expand any living accommodation included in the business. The value of a retail business is determined by the answers to a series of questions:

- Is this a good location for this retail business?
- Can customers park easily, safely and legally? Can the car parking be extended? Is it likely to be reduced by future road changes or parking regulations?
- Is there a flow of customers throughout the day? (Watch the store from a discreet distance and find out.)
- What local amenities are nearby? Pub, library, transport?
- How visible is the store?
- How many square metres of sales space are there? Can the sales space be expanded?
- What is the condition of the premises and any accommodation that goes with it?
- What is the value of the freehold or lease, and what are the terms of the lease? Remember that values vary from one geographical area to another.
- What is the condition of the store's display or trading equipment?
- What is the profitability of the business?
- What is the potential of the business? Could you add extra services (eg dry cleaning, lottery terminal) to broaden the store's appeal?

> "What is the potential of the business? Could you add extra services (eg dry cleaning, lottery terminal) to broaden the store's appeal?"

- What do people buy and how long are they in the store?
- What is the spread of goods on offer? Successful convenience stores offer a wide range of products, but a relatively narrow range of brands.
- What are the accounts telling you (see Chapter 1, pages 27–35)? Remember, as a buyer your understanding of value is based on what is included and shown in the accounts, not what is left out.

As you begin to focus on a particular business, and to read the accounts in detail, keep it in mind that with all types of business there is scope for changing profits by altering buying and selling policies. This might mean opening for longer or different hours to sell more effectively, or sourcing produce and goods from different suppliers or buying groups in order to buy more efficiently.

Make sure that you are equipped with the right kind of questions. Ask questions widely among retailers in your area (rather than in the area in which you plan to do business), and see if you can benefit from their experience.

It may be possible to approach trade associations and local business groups with the same questions:

- What are the main problems in starting out in your own business?
- What would you do differently now from when you started in your own business?
- What are the most and least profitable areas of your business?
- How can you get the best out of a business agent?
- How do you handle suppliers? How do you get trade credit?
- What associations should you belong to?

> "...as you visit the business you plan to buy, make sure you put any questions you have direct to the vendor and/or the agent."

Armed with this knowledge as you visit the business you plan to buy, make sure you put any questions you have direct to the vendor and/or the agent. It is important to ask direct questions from an informed point of view; you don't know it all, but you certainly do not want to appear to know nothing as you look round the businesses that interest you:

- What local conditions apply and on what days?
- Who are the customers? Where do they come from?
- Where can you add value?
- What is the store's market and what is your target market?
- What is the competition and where is it?
- How can this business balance what is popular with what is different?
- What is the image of this shop? Can you change it? Do you need to change it?

You will, of course, need to see the retailer's Profit and Loss Account. Remember that their transport, borrowing and utilities bills may well be radically different from yours. If you need clarification about any figures in the accounts, just ask. You may be able to see suppliers' invoices; these will help you analyse the costs you are taking on and give you some idea of the way in which the retailer has stocked the shop. For some people, the ideal is to find a relatively run-down or stagnant retail business at the right price.

> **"Have a formal Valuation Report made of the business and its assets, including a full Structural Survey of its premises and their condition…"**

As you look at the price the vendor is asking for the business, you should do the following:

- Have a formal Valuation Report made of the business and its assets, including a full Structural Survey of its premises and their condition (see Appendix 3).
- Check over the vendor's accounts.
- Look closely at how the profits are expressed.
- Determine what is paid in business rates.
- Ask the vendor for a copy of his last stocktake report. This will provide an indication of the value of the stock held (at cost price).

- Determine how many years of annual pre-tax profits the asking price represents. For example, a business with annual pre-tax profits of £50,000 which is selling for £150,000 is selling at three times profits. You should then find out whether this is typical for that specific retail sector. This may vary by location. You should ask a business agent.

Clearly, the retailer's relationship with customers is paramount as profits come from goods sold and services provided to them. Another vital area is the retailer's relationship with suppliers; profits can be increased through intelligent buying. Retailers can source their goods from many suppliers, from one supplier or from a combination of local, regional and national arrangements. If you have a relatively small turnover, cash and carry wholesalers allow you to buy smaller quantities. If you have a larger turnover, there are great advantages in belonging to a trading or buying group. These include the following:

> *"Retailers can source their goods from many suppliers, from one supplier or from a combination of local, regional and national arrangements."*

- Special promotions at low prices.
- Branded goods under the group's own label (eg NISA, Londis, Spar).
- All goods delivered.
- Trading advice.
- Shopfitting advice.
- Marketing campaigns and promotional material.

Freehold, leasehold and franchise

You will find retail businesses for sale under several different arrangements. The most common of these are freehold and leasehold, with some being franchise (see

Appendix 2). All have different advantages for the retailer, and all are worth considering.

Remember, if the business you're thinking of buying is housed in freehold premises it is usually possible, after you have bought it, to write an occupational lease. This would enable you to sell the freehold element as an investment and recoup a substansial part of your original outlay.

Key ratios

- *Ratio of staff costs to turnover* – in a convenience/ food store or CTN business, staff costs (including your own and your family's wages/income) should be a maximum of 8–10% of turnover.
- *Ratio of net profit to turnover* – this will be dependent on the retail sector you are operating in, but as a general rule you should be looking to achieve a net profit of at least 10% of turnover.
- *Weekly sales per square metre of the trading area* – you should be looking to achieve at least £80 per square metre per week in a higher-volume retail business such as food, off-licence or newsagency. In lower-volume, higher-margin businesses, you should be seeking to achieve £40–50 per square metre or more.

> *"In lower-volume, higher-margin businesses, you should be seeking to achieve £40–50 per square metre or more."*

- *Rental levels* – in respect of leasehold businesses, you should ensure that the rent is no more than the market rent for that location. You may wish to take specialist advice on this from a surveyor or at least obtain sales particulars from business agents for comparable retail units in the same area.

Top tips

- Be flexible about opening hours.
- Appoint dependable staff.
- Get an in-store ATM (cash point machine) – this will draw people in who are then likely to spend some of the cash in your shop.
- Concentrate on keeping your profit margins as high as possible.
- Use manufacturers' displays.
- Use the early settlement terms offered by some suppliers.
- Keep the store clean.

Notes

1. Consult publications such as *Convenience Store*, *The Grocer*, *Retail Newsagent*, *Retail Week*, and *Independent Retail News*.
2. British Retail Consortium.
3. British Retail Consortium.
4. March 2000: 18,393. Figures fluctuate. Consignia (formerly The Post Office) also includes 12,000 employees, £1.2 billion turnover and 25% of all cash transactions in the UK, and offers four services: Post Office Limited, Royal Mail, Parcelforce Worldwide, Subscription Services Limited. Post Office Limited (POL) (formerly Post Office Network and previously Post Office Counters Ltd) controls and runs the post office franchise in the UK. POL provides specialist training for new sub-postmasters, usually at the business and usually lasting around one week. A sub-postmastership does not automatically transfer with either the premises or the business. POL requires an application form, Cash Flow Plan and Business Plan.
5. See *Cabinet Office Performance & Innovation Unit Report*, 10.4.00.
6. Benefit Agency, National Savings, British Telecom, Giro banking services; also currency, travellers' cheques, travel insurance, passport forms, vehicle licensing.
7. Morgan Stanley Dean Witter retail survey, 1998.
8. Analysis from Christie & Co, 2000.
9. David Turner, Group Property Director, T&S Stores, 1999.

retail – a case study
Martin Connelly: newsagency, Tullibody

t is not always straightforward to identify the type of retail business you are looking for at the right price. To do so prospective buyers often have to pursue a number of different avenues in their search for a business, according to retailer Martin Connelly. When he bought his first shop, a 40 sq m newsagency in Tullibody, Clackmannanshire, Scotland, he scoured local newspapers, registered with specialist agents such as Christie & Co and even knocked on doors asking people if they might be interested in selling their shop. Although his door-knocking produced some openings, he got better results from dealing with an agent.

"Part of the agent's job is to assess the business, go through the accounts with the vendor and then discuss what the business is worth. In many cases vendors who use a specialist agent will be more sensible when it comes to value, thus saving me from wasting my time looking at businesses where the owners have unrealistic expectations," said Mr Connelly, who owns six shops.

He has built up his business by having a clear idea of what he's looking for: a business where the current owners have been in charge for a number of years, where there has been little change in product range, opening hours have not been extended and there is scope to improve the business. When he bought the Tullibody shop, turnover was £3,400 a week; when he leased it out, it was £17,000 a week.

Finding funding for his first purchase was relatively easy. It was when he came to buy his second property that he experienced problems. While banks were keen to assist with his first purchase, they were wary about whether he was capable of running two units. However, the sale of his second shop enabled him to fund his further purchases out of equity.

> "While banks were keen to assist with his first purchase, they were wary about whether he was capable of running two units."

"The first week in the business was nerve wracking. You are keen to please everybody and make sure the existing trade and goodwill don't disappear," he recalled. "But most of all you are anxious that the turnover at the end of the day and at the end of the week will meet your projections."

After that Martin Connelly set about identifying how to build up the business and where the growth would come from. In his view, you will not get a clear idea of how it can be developed until you are behind the counter. It is only then that you see what your customers are buying and listen to their views on what they would like to see on offer.

To attract more customers into the shop, he added 3 metres of magazine fixtures; he introduced milk and widened the range of confectionery on offer and added new product ranges. In the years since he bought his first shop, Martin Connelly says he has made only one mistake: buying a franchise convenience store, which was substantially less profitable than his newsagencies. The biggest mistake he sees other people making is having too high expectations of the growth they can achieve.

"They think that if they put in new fixtures and fittings and paint the premises, they will achieve growth. But first you have to clarify the accounts and ensure the business is generating the turnover the owners say it is. Then you look at the potential for improvement, but you have to remember that you can't force people to buy what they don't want to buy," he said.

Martin Connelly's tips

- The three most important things are still location, location and location.
- Have a clear understanding of the kind of business you want to buy.
- Don't take the owner's word on the turnover – do your own research on where customers come from and what they buy. Investigate nearby competitors.
- Don't fool yourself that you can build a dream – if the shop isn't in the right location and there isn't sufficient customer demand, no matter how much money you plough into it, it won't work.
- Spend time looking for your business and be realistic about what it can achieve.
- Remember that good staff are the key to your success.
- Keep a constant eye on how the retail market is changing and developing.

nine

How to buy
a care business

An introduction to the care market. Regulation. Are you right for the care business? Is this the right care home for you? Legal requirements.

An introduction to the care market

Of the 59.24 million people in the UK, 9.3 million (or 15.7%) are over 65. In 1900 there were 4.8% over 65; in 1938, 8.6%; and in 1980, 15.1%, so we are living longer and expect to live even longer. Life expectancy at birth in 2000 for men is 74.5 and for women 79.8.[1] (See page 184.) In 2000 a 60-year-old man can expect to live to 78.8, and a 60-year-old woman to 82.6.[2] This in turn means that more people are living in residential care homes, nursing homes, specialist homes or sheltered accommodation, often with age-related conditions and frailties.

There is a need for a range of homes to deliver the required nursing, residential and specialist care. Specialist care homes provide care for residents with special physical and/or psychological needs.[3] All types of home, which from April 2002 are known as "care homes",[4] will have to be registered with the appropriate regional office of the National Care Standards Commission. They are part of an industry where total spending, both public and private, is over £40 billion each year.[5] There are currently four major categories of care-home operator: national care groups; established regional and local operators (including small geographical monopolies), single-unit operators, and specialist providers:

- *National care groups* – traditionally, these operate purpose-built homes in terms of accommodation. They are expert in the market, have the advantage of economies of scale and, because of the quality of their buildings, are more likely to comply readily with new and changing care standards.
- *Regional/local operators* – these operators will

probably have a small chain; they will certainly have a strong local reputation under-pinned by local and regional contacts.

- *Single-unit operators* – private owners of a single care home.
- *Specialists* – these are homes that specialise either in the kind of clients they serve or in the kind of services they offer.

Whatever your ambitions in the care sector, you must know and meet the requirements of the Care Standards Act 2000. This governs the welfare of residents and their needs, the working environment, staffing, management and administration across a range of areas. For each area it covers – home, health and personal care, daily life and social activities, complaints and protection, environment, staffing, management and administration – the Act sets out minimum standards. The Care Standards Act[6] is required reading for aspiring care home owners.

> *"You can own a care business without having medical or nursing experience or qualifications; but you cannot operate one without qualifications."*

You can own a care business without having medical or nursing experience or qualifications; but you cannot operate one without qualifications. Under Standard 31 of the National Minimum Care Standards issued under the 2000 Care Standards Act, the registered manager of a care business must have the following:

- At least two years' experience in senior management of a care home within the last five years.
- In addition, a qualification at level 4 NVQ in management and care or its equivalent; or, in a nursing home, qualification as a first-level registered nurse together with a relevant management qualification.

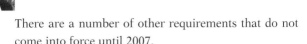

There are a number of other requirements that do not come into force until 2007.

Many buyers have no care experience, but there are plenty of roles in a care business that they can fulfil other than that of manager – taking on the accounts, maintenance, garden upkeep, resident activities and so on. But an understanding of care basics is essential for any owner. This is a complex (although not complicated) area which is rightly heavily regulated because vulnerable lives could be at risk. The regulation is intended to set out and enforce guidelines for the standards and care of residents. The regulatory bodies charged with inspecting homes have wide powers and can impose stringent penalties. This highly developed regulatory structure should not deter you if you want to own or run a care business. Everyone else in the same business has to adhere to the same standards as you.

> *"There is a range of opportunities emerging for the private operator as Local Authorities in the UK continue to outsource care provision."*

Around 70% of turnover in the care market derives from contracts with public bodies which are themselves both clients and regulation enforcers. Some run their own care homes, and are even competing providers. The market is affected by changes in NHS provision, by legislation and enforcement of new standards, by fluctuations in public-sector funding and by the performance of pension funds. However, private operators can, and do, prosper in it.

There is a range of opportunities emerging for the private operator as Local Authorities in the UK continue to outsource care provision. To take one example, in the USA care chains have developed hotel communities for the elderly – a midway phase for many people between remaining in their own homes and going into a nursing home. In Australia and elsewhere a similar concept is the retirement village, which provides a wide range of occupational activities. These cultural, economic and demographic changes are all taking place within a context where individuals are taking responsibility for their retirement. The care market will become increasingly complex and anyone entering as an investor, owner, operator or any combination of these needs to look at the actual and potential trading performance of the business.

There are several trends that point the way for the next few years. First, numbers of single rooms with en suite facilities are increasing fast to meet the new accommodation standards; secondly, there is a gradual increase in the quality of the majority of care homes; thirdly, there are increasingly more purpose-built new homes; and, fourthly, there is greater specialisation in the market as a whole.

In comparison with other property-based businesses, the return on capital in the care sector can be relatively high. A good care business should provide a return on capital invested within between four and six years, before tax, depreciation, loan repayments and bank charges. This means that return on capital might average 20% over five years.

The best way to plan your entry into the sector is to read widely and carefully in the sector's press and on web sites. Current examples of publications include *Caring Times*, *This Caring Business* and *Community Care Market News* (published by Laing & Buisson), plus the various directories published each year by both Fitzhugh and Laing & Buisson.[7] There are many other sources of information – including public bodies, associations, charities and Local Authorities – that help people

> *"A good care business should provide a return on capital invested within between four and six years, before tax, depreciation, loan repayments and bank charges."*

to choose a care home as a resident.[8] Most social services departments offer some sort of seminar or introductory course for new entrants to the industry. All this information can be of great use to you as you build up your picture of the sector. Also, speak to one or more current operators and a specialist business agent, and visit a broad range of care homes. As you become more familiar with the care environment and as you start to ask more searching questions about each business, your sense of what you want will emerge.

Regulation

Regulation has become – in principle at least – more transparent nationally and less complicated. In 2000 the Government announced its conclusions relating to physical standards in residential and nursing homes. This took the form of the Care Standards Act, which followed consultation with care users and suppliers[9] and will be enforced across the UK from 2002 by the National Care Standards Commission. Reading this book is no substitute for reading the Act itself and becoming aware of the National Minimum Care Standards issued under its authority. Section 5 (standards 19–26) sets out the standards that may have an impact on the layout of the buildings you are about to buy. Here are some examples of care standards which might have a considerable influence on the value of a care home:[10]

- 20.1: The home provides sitting, recreational and dining space ... apart from service users' private accommodation and excluding corridors and entrance hall amounting to at least 4.1m² for each service user. To be applied from 1 April 2007 for homes existing prior to 1 April 2002 which do not meet this standard.
- 23.2: In all new build, extensions and first time registrations, all places are provided in single rooms

with a minimum of 12m² usable floorspace (excluding en suite facilities).

- 23.3: Single rooms in current use have at least 10m² usable floor space (excluding en suite facilities) from 1 April 2007.
- 23.11: From 1 April 2007, existing homes that do not already provide 80% of places in single rooms must do so.

These standards relate to the physical environment of the care business, and affect all homes for the elderly. Existing homes which do not meet these space standards but which are nonetheless of good quality will have to change, and all care homes will have to conform to these standards by 2007. Until then, those properties with a high proportion of large single rooms and en suite bathrooms will be most likely to succeed in what has become a competitive market.

The Care Standards Act 2000 is tough and carries stiff penalties for non-compliance. Those in breach of it will face either criminal prosecution or cancellation of registration. Those who are unfit to be in the business will not and should not be in it. There may be a period of uncertainty as the Act is interpreted, and there may be a series of whistle-blowing cases as employees report abuses. However, during any period of change and transition, opportunities present themselves and good investments can be made.

> *"However, during any period of change and transition, opportunities present themselves and good investments can be made."*

There are other important pieces of legislation that affect the care sector. The National Minimum Wage and the Working Time Directive both have an impact on staffing costs and on the staffing availability in care homes. Periodic shortages of qualified nurses exacerbate staffing problems and many operators in the industry

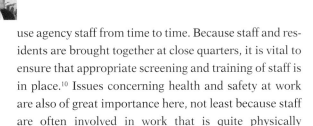

use agency staff from time to time. Because staff and residents are brought together at close quarters, it is vital to ensure that appropriate screening and training of staff is in place.[10] Issues concerning health and safety at work are also of great importance here, not least because staff are often involved in work that is quite physically demanding.

Are you right for the care business?

By definition, the care business deals with people who are either old or require specialist care. A good care business always puts the interests of its residents first. It is crucial that the right culture and ethos should come from those who own and manage a care home. By providing a service of the highest quality, integrity and humanity, a care business will prosper. But this is not a sector for those who wish to exploit others for ready gains or take advantage of others' hardships and difficulties.

You must distinguish between owning and running a care business. If you are an owner, you can, of course, take a more dispassionate view of the business and operate it as commercially as possible within the care environment. If you are an owner–manager, you will be closer to the everyday concerns of your residents – some of which may well be personally distressing and upsetting – and, at the same time, you will be charged with looking after the welfare not only of your residents but also that of your staff, your business and your family.

> *"It is crucial that the right culture and ethos should come from those who own and manage a care home."*

There is no typical care business owner or operator, but you should have a commitment to the industry and to its principles as well as the capacity to own, manage and run your own business. It might help to list the qualities that you would look for in a care home and match them to your own strengths in business and as a professional carer. Most of all, it is important to decide what you want from the care sector before you enter it. Do you want to build a chain of care homes over the next 5 or 10 years? Do you want to concentrate on building high-quality homes? Are you prepared to sell a care home with long-term residents? How much profit do you plan to take? How much are you prepared to re-invest? These are commercial decisions which you must make with investors, partners or family before you enter the business.

Is this the right care home for you?

Before you think of buying a particular care home it is essential to research the key areas that affect the business. As with any business, these areas are straight-forward and quantifiable. You must be thorough and persistent in your enquiries; these must include a thorough survey of the building and valuation of the business (see Appendix 3).

Here, your knowledge of the care sector is vital, and the help of a good business agent will be of great value. You should have a clear idea about what is normal for the sector, both in terms of what a home does for its residents, and also in terms of the profits a home delivers for its owner. Industry research shows that nursing homes tend to be larger (40 beds average) than care homes (21 beds average). A net profit of around 25% of the fee income is average for the care sector; nursing homes tend to produce profits of 20–25%, and care homes a profit of 30–35%. Staffing costs (55–65% of fee income) tend to be higher where more experienced or qualified staff are required.[11] You must decide how your prospective home fits that pattern, and how the figures might change when you take over. Armed with your sense of what is normal and expected within the sector, you will be better placed to look objectively at the home or homes you have in mind.

In your approach you should be thorough and realistic, and you should keep things simple. It is helpful to divide your questions into those which concern the external affairs of the home – essentially its market – and those which concern the internal workings of the home. Your research should begin with these questions:

- What are the local demographics? Will the home have sufficient residents in coming years?
- What is the local and regional competition? Are any new developments planned nearby?
- What is the location of the home and what is its prime catchment area – socially, financially and physically? An urban home will have a greater catchment population and may be easier for both staff and relatives than a rural one – travel to the home is a possible problem in rural areas. At the same time, homes in urban areas may face greater competition.
- What kind of Local Authority is it? What is its funding history? Does it run care homes of its own?

> "What is the location of the home and what is its prime catchment area – socially, financially and physically?"

There are many aspects of the home you must look into; you have the business to consider, the premises to assess, the staff to oversee, the Local Authority to liaise with, the legislation to meet and, above all, the residents to look after. It pays to be thorough and to ask as many questions as you can before the purchasing process begins. There are fundamentals that you must consider:

- Is the business freehold or leasehold?
- Is this business part of a chain of care homes?
- Are there good management accounts and cash flow figures?
- What are the figures for historical and current occupancy levels? (See "Key ratios" at the end of this

chapter.) Occupancy levels tend to vary, but 85%[12] is an acceptable minimum, unless you have little or no debt, in which case lower occupancies are acceptable. If the occupancy levels are lower than you think they should be, find out why.

- What are the fees? How much does it cost to stay here? What is included in the fees?
- What are the staff costs? Does the registered manager have the appropriate qualifications? How do regulations governing expert staff and staff/resident ratios affect your staff costs and therefore your profits?
- What are the proportions of privately funded and publicly funded residents? How many referrals are there from the Local Authority/Area Health Authority? Both these figures may be subject to rapid change.

> *"Occupancy levels tend to vary, but 85% is an acceptable minimum, unless you have little or no debt..."*

- What is the percentage of single rooms and those with en suite bathrooms? What are the sizes of these rooms? Are you going to have to convert some double rooms to single-room occupancy to comply with the new regulations? What are the dimensions of the public areas?
- How good are the access, parking and facilities for visitors and staff?
- What are the costs of improving the fabric and decorations of the building? What inconvenience will this cause to the residents?
- Is there scope for structural improvements or an extension?

Then there are matters concerning the regulatory record and background of the home. These affect its operation and are of the highest importance:

- Is the home registered as a residential care home or as a nursing home, or as both?
- What does the inspection report[13] tell you? These are publicly available and usually published twice a year. They cover such matters as registration, admissions, discharges, deaths, fees, the condition of the buildings, the comfort of the residents, environmental health, fire safety, health care, staffing, staff structure, training, supervision, and the experience of residents – including their privacy, dignity, independence, choice and rights. There may also be a summary and assessment from a lay assessor, which will provide a non-technical account of life in the home.

There are also questions of culture and business style which relate to how the home is run both as a residence and as a business. You will not find answers to these questions from a cursory visit or from superficial enquiries. It takes time and effort to find out what you need to know, but you should not proceed without asking the following:

- Is the service of high quality? Could it be higher?
- Is the attitude of staff professional and friendly?
- Are there any problems that can be solved with further investment? Are there any that can be solved without the need for further investment?

You should also have in mind the physical environment of the home:

- Does the home already comply with the required standards? Are the public areas, corridors, lifts (if any) and lavatories suitable for disabled people and wheelchair access? If not, what costs will be incurred to achieve compliance and re-registration?
- Is the home well equipped and well maintained?

- What are the kitchens like: commercial or domestic standard?
- What are the laundry facilities like? Are there industrial machines?
- Can you extend or add value to the facilities or the provision?
- Is the owner's or manager's accommodation in good order?

As you consider the location, background, style and fabric of the home, put yourself in the position of a resident or resident's family. How do you feel about this home? What do you notice? Could you offer anything that makes this home different from others of a similar kind in the area? As you narrow your search, you should expect to see the business accounts and the most recent inspection reports.[15] The management of the home should be able to do the following:

> *"...put yourself in the position of a resident or resident's family. How do you feel about this home? What do you notice?"*

- Understand how the private sector and the NHS operate.
- Anticipate, respond to and comply with changes in care legislation.
- Run the business cost effectively.
- Inspire trust in residents and Local Authorities.
- Keep up to date clinically.
- Keep up to date technologically and be prepared to use new software.
- Relate well to residents and their families.
- Be keen to integrate the home into the local community and to establish the home as a community of its own.

Staff and residents together provide the continuity that makes up the day-to-day life of a care home. The first moment you cross the threshold of a care home as a potential buyer, you should be aware that this may be the start of your career as an owner. You need to behave with great courtesy and circumspection. Your purchase may depend on the future plans you have for the business. Here are some guidelines about what you need to consider when introducing changes to the services you offer:

> *"Join in the community whenever you can. For example, have open days, garden parties and fêtes."*

- Listen to your residents and their families, and act on their views when you can.
- Be aware that any upgrading of the buildings may need to take place gradually, not only because of financial or logistical concerns but also because change can be emotionally disruptive to residents.
- Maintain and build on the contacts of the previous owner and make sure you have a good relationship with your Area Health Authority, your Local Authority and those who are responsible for referring people to the home.
- Monitor occupancy levels and staff costs above all else.
- Appoint good staff and train them.
- Market your business to the referring agencies (organisations that refer potential clients to your home) and through surgeries, libraries, churches and charities.
- Join in the community whenever you can. For example, have open days, garden parties and fêtes.
- Arrange programmes of activities, visits, talks and outings for the residents.
- Monitor your local competition.

It is important that the life of the home – its residents, staff, contractors and suppliers – should be continuous and not disrupted by the sale. You can work with the vendor and the agent to ensure this happens. It may mean working for the vendor or asking them to work for you during a period of adjustment. In this way, everyone may benefit.

Legal requirements

As with any business which offers goods and services to the public, there are statutory obligations concerning planning, environmental health, safety, fire regulations, building regulations, public liability insurance and employees' rights (see Appendix 1). As a care home is often subject to scrutiny, it is particularly important to have all the legal checks and balances in place. It is

> *"As a care home is often subject to scrutiny, it is particularly important to have all the legal checks and balances in place."*

crucial that matters of risk management, responsibility and insurance (on and off the site) have been thought about by the owner.

Key ratios

- *Ratio of staff costs to turnover* – nursing approximately 55–60%; residential 48–50%.
- *Ratio of profit to turnover* – nursing approximately 25%; residential 30%.
- *Sale price as a multiple of adjusted net profit* – the industry norm is to multiply adjusted net profit by four to six times to give the value of the business, or its sale price.
- *Occupancy rates* (the percentage of rooms occupied by residents over any given period) – 85% is an acceptable minimum.

Top tips

- Maintain a good relationship with your inspector.
- Keep up to date with changes in equipment.

- Arrange special events for the residents; for example, trips, visits, talks, events, birthday parties.
- Encourage relatives to visit regularly and informally.
- Have the business reviewed occasionally by an agent.
- Network locally.
- Never allow care standards to slip.
- Train and re-train your staff.

Notes

1. The Office for National Statistics, UK figures 1998; The Economist, *World in Figures*, 2000 (based on UK figures 1997).

2. Office for National Statistics.

3. Homes for those with learning disabilities, mental illness, brain injury, drug and alcohol addiction and so on, not necessarily for the elderly.

4. As of April 2002, all homes are registered with and monitored by the National Care Standards Commission at a regional level. Headquarters, Newcastle upon Tyne. Regional offices: London (London and South East regions); Nottingham (Trent region); Darlington (Northern and Yorkshire region); Preston (North West region); Cambridge (Eastern region); Taunton (South West region) and Birmingham (West Midlands region).

5. *Fitzhugh Directory*, 1999–2000. Spending on long-term healthcare is around £14 billion, £9 billion of which is residential.

6. Published by, and available from, the Stationery Office (www.thestationeryoffice.com) and its agents. See also www.hmso.gov.uk/acts.htm.

7. See Laing & Buisson's *Carehome Information on CD-Rom*, *Healthcare Directory* (annual), *Assisted Living Markets* (annual), www.laingbuisson.co.uk; also *Counsel & Care – The Choice is Yours* (report).

8. There is a wealth of good-quality information in the medical library of the King's Fund.

9. See 1998 Government White Paper, *Modernising Social Services*, and Department of Health consultation document, *Fit For The Future? National Required Standards for Residential and Nursing Homes for Older People*.

10. See National Minimum Standards, Care Standards Act 2000, section 6 and 7 (standards 27–30, 31–38).

11. Christie & Co figures, 2000.

12. Christie & Co figures, 2000.

13. Compiled from one pre-arranged and one unannounced inspection.

care – a case study
Huw James: Redwood Healthcare plc, Barnt Green, Worcs.

When Huw James bought his first home, the 45-registration Brookdale Nursing Home in Kidderminster, he set himself several criteria.

The first was location, or more specifically a home which was close to his own home. The second was size – 25-plus registrations for a residential home and 35-plus for a nursing home. His theory was that he would experience the same fixed administration costs regardless of the size of the home; compliance with legislation, necessary repairs and breakdowns. "A lift is just as likely to break down in a 10-bedroom home as in a 30-bedroom one," he reasons.

The third criterion was that the home had to be trading successfully. To determine whether it was, the accounts were scrutinised. Figures for current occupancy levels, fee income and wages were used to indicate what the staffing requirements would be. "You have to decide what you think staff should be paid and therefore what your staff costs will be. As labour is the biggest single cost in the care sector, you need to monitor these costs very carefully, which is why we monitor all our costs on a weekly basis," said Mr James.

Before buying a home, he also looks carefully at the surrounding area and at the competition, to gauge how the local market may develop in the future. Finally, he takes into account the quality of the building – not just the bricks and mortar, but whether it will be able to satisfy the existing regulations and any anticipated changes in standards.

> *"He advised other buyers not to be nervous about making repeat visits and cautioned against believing everything they are told by the vendor..."*

During his previous career helping others to acquire care businesses, one thing surprised him about many first-time buyers – how little they visited the business they were proposing to buy. "Every time you go, you see something you missed the last time and you get a better feel for how the business is operating. Deals can take several months to complete, and during that time staff may leave, new people may be employed at terms and conditions you would not have agreed to or there may be a new inspection report you didn't know about. You need to keep your finger on the pulse," he said. He advised other buyers not to be nervous about making repeat visits and cautioned against believing everything they are told by the vendor, for example about the size of the rooms – a critical factor with the new standards specifying a minimum of 10 sq m for existing homes.

His favourite piece of advice is that the best deal you do may be the one you didn't do. For example, he knows of at least two first time buyers who outbid him by a substantial amount to acquire homes they later sold for much less than they paid. "In these cases, they didn't really look at what they were buying and lived to regret it. If you set yourself tight criteria which make it difficult to find something which fits, you might persuade yourself to settle for less," Mr James said. "Some people think the care market is a licence to make money, but it isn't."

Funding has not been a problem for Huw James, who had built up a group of 10 homes eight years after acquiring his first property. He believes that if buyers have chosen their business well, done their homework thoroughly and presented their proposal and themselves well, lenders will be keen to back them.

Huw James's tips

- Look carefully at the business you are proposing to buy and play devil's advocate.
- Ask lots of questions of the vendors.
- Don't be afraid of looking stupid – your questions may not be as silly as you think.
- Make sure the business you are buying complies with all the regulations and national standards – or can be adapted to comply with them.
- Make sure you have correctly calculated what your return on your investment will be.
- Bear in mind that the costs you are given may not be accurate if the home is not complying with the Staffing Notice.
- Check if the owner and their family are working in the business and take into account their labour in your calculations of staff costs.

ten

How to buy a childcare business

*A*n introduction to the childcare market. Are you right for the children's day nursery business? Is this children's day nursery the right one for you? Financial aspects. Service, marketing and publicity. Legal requirements.

An introduction to the childcare market

Although the average annual population growth in the UK between 1990 and 2000 was 0.22%, there is a falling number of under-5s in the UK. If you look more closely, however, the figures reveal a definite trend. There are 3.67 million (6.2% of the population) aged from 1 to 5, but there are only around 1.6 million childcare places available for them.[1] (See page 200.)

Most importantly for childcare operators, an increasing number of women – who traditionally care for children at home – are working. As lifestyles and demographics change,[2] the need for provision of childcare will increase.

There are several categories of nursery or home-based childcare for the under-5s. These include nannies (who look after one or more children in the child's home); childminders (who look after one or more children in the childminder's home); playgroups; Local Education Authority day nurseries and nursery schools; Local Education Authority pre-school classes; private children's day nurseries; and nurseries at work – usually provided by a company for its employees' children. Together, they cover the five main ways in which care is offered. The categories within the sector and its regulatory structure are as follows:

- Full daycare.
- Sessional daycare.
- Crèches.
- Out-of-school care.
- Childminding.

This chapter is concerned with private day nurseries. The number of private day nurseries increased by 381% between 1987 and 1997.[3] During this period the places provided by those nurseries increased by 457% to around 172,000. Nevertheless, there is still a shortfall in nursery places and therefore tremendous scope for greater expansion in this sector.

In many ways there are similarities between the nursery sector and the care home sector: both need businesses that are intensive in staff and time, and that provide care environments. In the nursery sector, correspondingly, there are large operators with chains of nurseries, middle-sized operators, and private owner–operators all providing varieties of childcare. The market share of all the major chains, however, is still only around 10%.[4] This is changing as many corporate operators are expanding by new-build development complemented by the acquisition of privately owned children's nurseries. Other business models are evolving as day nurseries form networks to exchange information, share difficulties, negotiate for bulk discounts with suppliers or share the cost of consultants.

> *"Nevertheless, there is still a shortfall in nursery places and therefore tremendous scope for greater expansion in this sector."*

Children's day nurseries are local businesses that are nationally regulated. The Office for Standards in Education (OFSTED) is responsible for regulating and inspecting childminders and daycare providers from eight regional offices.[5] Under the Children Act 1989 as amended by the Care Standards Act 2000, OFSTED will inspect all childcare provision. National Standards[6] set by the Department for Education and Skills will cover such things as the following:

- The suitability of adults to care for children.
- The ratio of adults to children.

- Space.
- Resources.
- Activities to develop children's emotional, physical, intellectual and social capabilities.
- Safety.
- Equipment and toys.
- Health and infection control.
- Equality of opportunity for all children.
- Special needs.
- The management of children's behaviour.
- Partnership with parents and carers.
- Child protection procedures.
- Records.

Any new applications for registration of a childcare business must be made to OFSTED, which provides information for care providers and parents on a range of issues including inspection reports and publications. There are also several affiliated organisations that can be reached through OFSTED.[7]

> "...usually about 80% of clients of a children's day nursery come from within five miles of the business."

The crucial statistic which any owner–operator or corporate operator cannot ignore is that usually about 80% of clients of a children's day nursery come from within five miles of the business. It is a vital local business and one that should be fairly easy to assess on local criteria. There are three markets that support children's nurseries:

- The local neighbourhood.
- The corporate market (including workplace nurseries which generate business from both employees and people who work close to the nursery).
- The commuting market (business generated from those who drop their children off en route to work).

The best way to familiarise yourself with the children's nursery sector, or to improve your knowledge of it, is to read widely and visit as many children's nurseries as you possibly can. Read brochures and look in directories. At any one time in the UK there may be 200 nurseries for sale across a range of age, provision, locality and price. You can talk to operators outside the area where you plan to buy, and you can glean a great deal of information by talking to OFSTED and visiting its web site, which holds its database of inspection reports. You can also read social services' reports for a range of nurseries. There is a great deal of information available from organisations such as the National Day Nursery Association, Pre-School Learning Alliance and Professional Association of Nursery Nurses. Currently, the main children's nursery periodicals are *Nursery World* and *Nursery Management Today*.

Are you right for the children's day nursery business?

Most people know whether they would like to work with children and many, as parents, have developed an affinity and rapport with them. The children's nursery business demands that natural impulses to care for and have fun with children are made into identifiable professional skills. These skills can be learned and improved with practice.

As a children's nursery owner you need to understand the business and to have a clear sense of what it means

> *"The children's nursery business demands that natural impulses to care for and have fun with children are made into identifiable professional skills."*

for your manager and staff to work with children all day. As an owner–manager you must be rigorous about the qualities you have, those you lack and those you want to acquire:

- What is your professional attitude? What do you think of as professional behaviour? Are you loyal, discreet and circumspect? Are you punctual, enthusiastic and polite? Are you knowledgeable but ready to add to that knowledge?
- How do you get on with children? Are you patient with them, willing to work well with them, listen to them, and speak to them so that they understand you? Do you have respect for, and sensitivity about, their wishes and needs?
- Are you able to work with parents? Can you listen to them, talk to them about their children, and be patient and approachable?
- Can you balance the running of the business with taking care of staff and, of course, looking after the children in your care?
- How are you at dealing with authority? You will need to comply with many regulations and standards that form the legislation governing the business. You will need to form a good relationship with your OFSTED inspector.
- Are you creative and do you have flair? Children consume ideas and you will need to work hard to keep the nursery intellectually fresh and lively.
- What are the ages of the children? Many children's nurseries cater for a wide age range, from as young as a few weeks to 4 or 5 years. You may find that there is a trend for older nursery children to go to school as national education policy encourages younger children to do this, and this may affect your profits.

Is this children's day nursery the right one for you?
Buying a children's day nursery means that you are buying a business which should produce income from the moment you take over. You have access to all the expertise, experience, knowledge and contacts of the business and its staff. However, you should look closely at why the business is for sale, calculate the cost of any

changes you may wish to make, and think carefully about whether the business itself or the market in the area could be expanded.

If you buy a childcare business, communication will be vital to its success – for example, with the following:

- Parents.
- Staff.
- Schools.
- Other children's nurseries.
- Regulatory bodies.
- Training colleges.
- Local community businesses, services, libraries, charities, social groups and so on.

The location of the nursery is of paramount importance, given that most of its business will come from nearby. Safe parking is vital. The site must be accessible and the buildings must be visible. There should be safety and security measures in place.

Children's nurseries can be converted domestic space, purpose-built or of modular construction such as Portakabins. Whatever the type, you should make sure that you have a professional survey of the buildings and a valuation of the

> *"Most important to the business are its staff. They should be friendly, professional and qualified. Equipment such as toys should be in good order..."*

business made. The buildings should be in good order, and ideally have spacious and warm rooms. Most important to the business are its staff. They should be friendly, professional and qualified. Equipment such as toys should be in good order and designed for different types of play and to improve co-ordination and muscle strength. An outdoor play area is essential in the summer, although children need fresh air all year round, of course. Ask about day trips and outings.

As you look around the business, look for signs that the children there have fun and enjoy themselves; look for a calm, welcoming and friendly atmosphere which derives from a sensible routine. Take into account the ages of the children. Ask yourself if a large proportion of them are about to leave for primary or infant school. Also ask about the style or concept of care and education provided (eg Montessori).

A good children's nursery might provide, or have plans to provide, the following facilities for its children:[8]

- Book corner.
- Computer.
- Construction.
- Cooking.
- Craft and woodwork.
- Dressing up.
- Gardening.
- Home corner.
- Investigative area.
- Malleable materials.
- Music and sound.
- Painting.
- Physical play.
- Table-top games.
- Water play.

> "There should be a well-thought-out curriculum, and behind that a set of principles and a commitment to a range of standards in the nursery."

Behind these physical provisions there should be a well-thought-out curriculum, and behind that a set of principles and a commitment to a range of standards in the nursery. Historically these standards derive from public national guidelines such as *Desirable Outcomes for Children's Learning on Entering Compulsory Education* (published by the

Qualifications and Curriculum Authority, 1996) or from other sources such as Local Authority guidelines or professional literature.[9] However, these standards are now regarded by some early learning experts as bad practice. Current thinking on early learning development and curriculum is encapsulated in the *Foundation Stage Six Early Learning Goals* (September 2000) in the following areas:

- Personal, social and emotional development.
- Communication, language and literacy.
- Mathematical development.
- Knowledge and understanding of the world.
- Physical development.
- Creative development.[10]

From September 2001 the legal standards have been set and enforced by OFSTED, which issues information and national standards on the full range of regulatory matters.

> *"There should be a good system in place to manage the cash flow of the business, collect fees and pay both staff and suppliers on time."*

Financial aspects

The accounts will give you the fees, income, profits and costs for the business. You will have to pay business rates and, in due course, your valuer may be able to re-negotiate with your Local Authority how much you pay. You should also ask for details of staff salaries and contracts, employment records and qualifications. There should be a good system in place to manage the cash flow of the business, collect fees and pay both staff and suppliers on time.

A valuation should be based on the business's accounts, with all personal expenses and allowances removed. These accounts should produce a figure for the earnings before any interest payments, income tax and depreciation.

The business may be offered as a freehold but many nurseries are operated from leasehold properties. This means that you will be taking on the tenancy of the buildings. Your solicitor should make clear your responsibilities under the lease and your liabilities over time. You should calculate for rent increases if these are part of your lease arrangement, and you should be clear about what repairs you must do and what repairs you may leave for the landlord (see Appendix 2 for more details on tenure).

Service, marketing and publicity

Bear in mind that this is a local business, and that both children and parents are your clients. You will need to make sure that you are personally engaged with all aspects of the business, and particularly with the children in your care and with their parents. Provide the kind of informed and intelligent service you might expect of anyone looking after your own children.

> *"Bear in mind that this is a local business… An important part of your marketing will be through word of mouth and personal recommendation…"*

An important part of your marketing will be through word of mouth and personal recommendation, and you will need to take the following steps:

- Keep the nursery areas bright and clean inside and out.
- Welcome prospective clients (parents) and give them as much of your time as they need.
- Write a short brochure setting out the advantages of the nursery, your particular approach to child-care and where to find you.
- Build relationships with local businesses who may need your services and with people such as residential house agents who are frequently asked about local schools and nursery facilities.

- Build relationships with local schools.
- Get involved in local events that are appropriate and safe for the children. Join in the community whenever you can; for example, have open days, garden parties and fêtes.
- Listen to parents and act on their views whenever you can.
- Appoint good staff, train them well and re-train them.
- Market the business to the referring agencies and through surgeries, libraries, churches and charities.

The legal requirements

As with any business that offers goods and services to the public, there are statutory obligations concerning planning, environmental health, safety, fire regulations, building regulations, public liability insurance and employees' rights (see Appendix 1, pages 204–5). As a children's day nursery is subject to public scrutiny, it is particularly important to have all the legal checks and balances in place.

The legislation that governs most of what you can do and how you must run your nursery is the Children Act 1989 as amended by the Care Standards Act 2000 and the Regulations and National Standards issued under it.[11] The 2000 Act makes requirements about matters such as space per child, staff ratios, administration, access to a safe outdoor area, hygiene, furniture, types and quality of toys and so on. These requirements may vary regionally because the 1989 Act was, until 2001, enforced by Local Authorities, which applied the Act through visits by their registration officers. It may be some time before the National Standards become properly consistent.

> *"As a children's day nursery is subject to public scrutiny, it is particularly important to have all the legal checks and balances in place."*

However, any childcare business should have historical records and policies on the following:

- Admissions and attendance records.
- Waiting lists.
- Staffing.
- Health and safety.
- Accident reporting and procedure.
- Hygiene.
- Security.
- Child welfare (including suspected child abuse).
- Rules for delivering and collecting children.
- Information and filing of reports.
- Behaviour and special needs.
- Health records.
- Contact and general practitioner details.

Key ratios

- *Ratio of turnover to net profit* – approximately 35% pre-rent.
- *Ratio of staff costs to turnover* – approximately 45–50%.

Top tips

- Assess things before you change them.
- Maintain a good relationship with your OFSTED inspector.
- Meet all staff, clients and suppliers, and develop good working relationships.
- Handle all new enquiries personally.
- Keep the nursery areas bright, clean and well maintained.

Notes

1. Greenhouse Childcare Consultancy figures in M Pace, *Starting a Nursery*, 1999, page 5.
2. Good-quality national demographic information is in the *Social Trends* series published by the Office for National Statistics; local demographic information is available from the Learning + Skills

Council, from the Small Business Service and from local residential house agents.

3. From 1,413 to 5,500 (*Independent Day Nursery Workforce Survey* published by the Local Authority Management Board, now The Standards Board for England, 1998).

4. M Pace, *Starting a Nursery*, page 8.

5. Headquarters, Newcastle upon Tyne. Regional offices: London (London and South East regions); Nottingham (Trent region); Darlington (Northern and Yorkshire region); Preston (North West region); Cambridge (Eastern region); Taunton (South West region) and Birmingham (West Midlands region).

6. See www.childcarelink.gov.uk

7. For example, National Childminding Association, Pre-School Learning Alliance, National Day Nursery Association, Kids' Clubs Network.

8. See *Managing Your Nursery*, by R Andreski and S Nicholls, 1997, pages 62–3.

9. For example *Nursery World, Nursery Management Today* magazines and *Setting Standards: A Guide for the Nursery Professional*, by R Andreski and S Nicholls. Public bodies include the British Association for Early Childhood Education, the Child Accident Prevention Trust, and the Qualifications and Curriculum Authority.

10. *Curriculum Guidance for the Foundation Stage*, Qualifications and Curriculum Authority, QCA/00/587 (www.qca.org.uk).

11. See *Day Care: Is it Right for You?* (OFSTED – HMI 284). For the national standards for daycare, see: Department of Education and Skills – DfEE 0487/2001, 0488/2001, 0489/2001, and 0490/2001. For inspection standards, see: *Inspecting Nursery Settings* (OFSTED – HMI 226).

Appendices

Statutory regulations and duties

For any business that offers goods and services to the public, there are statutory obligations concerning licensing, planning, environmental health, fire regulations, building regulations, public liability insurance and employees' rights. Whether your business is leasehold or freehold, you are obliged to meet a range of statutory requirements on these matters. The vendor should have the appropriate records relating to the business and property. These should include the following:

- Staff employment records. In most cases, you must honour staff contracts under legislation covered by the Transfer of Undertakings of Protection of Employment (TUPE). As a rule, a new owner is obliged to keep on the current staff and to honour their existing contracts of employment. However, there are some circumstances in which TUPE does not apply and you are advised to seek further advice on this complicated area from an employment specialist if you need more information.
- The planning of repairs and maintenance and a Maintenance Plan.
- Responsibilities under the Landlord and Tenant Act.
- Responsibilities under relevant access, leases, licences and agreements.
- Correspondence with the regulatory bodies concerned with planning, building regulations, health

and safety, environment and fire prevention (along with a Fire Certificate).[1] (See page 210.)

- Records of meetings with the landlord, although these may be subject to a rent-confidentiality agreement.
- Records of utilities and building services.
- Records of re-decoration and repair.
- Records of routine maintenance to equipment (eg gas safety certificates).
- Waste management.
- First-aid provision.
- Licences and certificates.
- Health and safety policy[2] covering the aims and responsibilities for managers, employees and safety representatives.
- Risk and hazard assessment.
- A recognised quality management system (where appropriate).

Many of these regulations change from time to time as new laws are passed in the UK and the EU.

Licensing for the hospitality trades

Before you start business in any of the licensed trades, you will need to make sure that you are up to date with the law.[3]

At the time of writing, licensed premises are subject to the 1964 Licensing Act. Its provisions are complex, covering 40 different kinds of licence or permission. Until any proposals for modernisation become law, the 1964 Licensing Act is still in force.

Under the 1964 Act any business that sells alcohol to the public must have a *Justices' Licence*. These licences are granted by special justices of the peace called licensing justices. These justices form a Licensing Committee which meets at least five times a year; the main meeting – the General Annual Licensing Meeting – is in February.

If you are buying a licensed business that is currently trading, it will already have the necessary licence or licences. An *On-Licence* entitles the holder to sell alcohol to be drunk either on or off the premises of a named public house; an *Off-Licence* entitles the holder to sell alcohol from a named premises, but only to be drunk off the premises. A *Part IV Licence* is required to sell alcohol in a hotel or guesthouse; special conditions apply, and these are available from the Clerk to the Licensing Justices at local Magistrates' Courts.

You must transfer the licence into your name when you buy a licensed business by applying to the Licensing Committee. For this to take place without interruption to the business you should apply for a *Protection Order* or an *Interim Authority*. It enables you to continue trading until the second licensing session after it is granted. You will have to satisfy the Licensing Committee that you intend to apply for a transfer of the existing Justices' Licence into your name and that you are a fit and proper person to hold a liquor licence. A licence can be jointly held, and this is a good option for husband–wife or partner ownership of a pub, restaurant or hotel.

It is increasingly common for magistrates to expect you to attend and complete courses organised by the British Institute of Innkeeping (BII) for the National Licensee's Certificate. The Certificate is not a statutory requirement for those wanting to hold a licence, but it would be imprudent to apply for one without it. Details of locally run courses are available from the BII.

You must, of course, transfer the licence into your own name as soon as possible. The transfer process is relatively simple.[4] The new licence in your name replaces the existing licence from the time of the transfer and is valid until the time at which the original licence would have expired.

Although transferring a licence from one landlord to another can be straightforward, it can sometimes be difficult to get a new licence (especially where the Licensing Committee feels that there are already enough licensed businesses in the area). Notice of an application for a new licence must be announced in the press and displayed at the premises. You also have to send a plan of the building to the Clerk to the Licensing Justices.[5]

Once you have a licence, you must comply with a complex set of rules governing hours, young people, rights of entry and your right to refuse and eject, gaming, betting, entertainment, weights and measures, prices, displayed notices, drinking and driving and violence.

While a Justices' On-Licence is key to the operation of a public house, there are a number of other licences that may be either desirable or necessary to operate certain businesses. For example, a restaurant or guesthouse may have a Part IV Licence (already mentioned), which permits the sale of alcohol for consumption with meals to residents and *bona fide* guests. A public house which has a restaurant area or which serves a significant amount of food may choose to apply for a *Section 68 Supper Hour Certificate*, which adds one hour to the general licensing hours for customers taking substantial refreshment. Where premises are altered to provide live music or other entertainment, an *Extended Hours Order* can be applied for, thereby extending permitted hours to 1 am. For businesses such as nightclubs where music and dancing are the main activities, a *Special Hours Certificate* can be granted, provided that there is also a *Public Entertainment Licence* in force and substantial refreshment is available.

If you wish to operate gaming machines in any business, these fall under the Gaming Act 1968. The rules are different for public houses and licensed clubs, with varying jackpot limits. For public houses a *Section 34 Permit* is required. This limits the number of machines that are allowed, and the level of jackpot payment which the machines can deliver.

Given that a licence you hold may have to change if you want to increase your trade, and that you may want a supplement to the licence,[6] you will need the advice of a licensing solicitor.

A *licensing solicitor* is an essential ally in any dealings with the Licensing Justices in obtaining or transferring a licence. You could find one simply by asking the local court's licensing department, by asking the vendor of the licensed business you are buying, by asking the vendor's agent, by asking your trade association or by asking other licensees. Choose your solicitor carefully, and make sure they are in court frequently enough to know the scene and stay on top of the law, and that they handle various types of licences, including yours. When the time comes for you to change or augment your licence, a licensing solicitor will look at your plans and give advice on any problems (and the solutions), the attitude of the local police force, and the legal requirements. Your solicitor should also be aware of any impending changes in legislation and local by-laws that may affect you. You can send in your application and turn up at court with the solicitor to outline your plans. Other circumstances that need public permission include extending your premises, extending the licensing hours, having dancing or musical performances, having tables and chairs outside, or installing gaming machines (Amusements With Prizes or AWPs).

Any application to change the licensing status of a pub, hotel, restaurant or off-licence will be considered by the Licensing Committee. The court dates are set out in February, the start of the licensing year; you can find out these dates at the court's licensing division. Normally, an application has to reach the court 21 days before the date on which the application will be heard. Work backwards from the date you wish to start operating your new business. Include time for the transfer sessions, the application itself, amassing material for the application, any preparation you need to do before you see your licensing solicitor and, of course, a margin of error in case things go wrong and have to be re-done.

You will need to provide a range of documents showing that you have the proper health and safety, fire, planning, and Local Authority consents as you proceed. The best place to find out about who needs what is *The Good Practice Guide*,[7] which is essentially a general policy document setting out the requirements of each licensing court.[8] Other authorities will need to be informed as the process moves forward; for example parish council, police, and Local Authority. Each will want to complete its own enquiry and it makes sense to enable them to do so by having the appropriate plans available. The various forms of consent required from Local Authority departments, police, fire service and parish council make up the complex background to your application.

Refer to your Business Plan to explain clearly and simply why you want to change your licence, what you want to do, and why you should be allowed to do it.

Applications to the Local Authorities for a Public Entertainment Licence (PEL) are assessed on the maximum number of people permitted on the premises. The cost of such a licence can vary enormously depending on where you are, cities and towns being generally more expensive than rural areas. If you involve the local fire officers, environmental health officers, police and highways department (for pavement permits) early on in your application process, you may save yourself expensive revisions later. Get their informal advice before you make any formal application or alteration.

Finally, you must also have two licences if you broadcast copyright material in the public areas of the business. These are the Performing Right Society (PRS) Licence and the Phonographic Performance Limited (PPL) Licence.[9]

Notes

1. See Fire Precautions Order 1988 and Fire Precautions Regulations 1992.

2. See Health & Safety at Work Act 1974 and the EU legislation Safety in the Workplace 1993–1996. There are also responsibilities to those who are visiting the premises – clients, technicians, builders, visiting professionals – and these are listed under the Occupier's Liability Acts 1957 and 1984.

3. The Home Office has a range of information, publications and advice. The British Institute of Innkeeping (BII) is a good source of information on current and forthcoming legislation. For advice and help with debt and financial hardship, the Society of Licensed Victuallers is a good resource; it is worth registering with this charity when you start business in the licensed trades.

4. For the transfer of a liquor licence you must give 21 days' notice to the Clerk to the Licensing Justices, Chief Police Officer, Local Authority, Town or Parish Council and the existing licensee. The licence is for a maximum of three years, renewable.

5. See *Handbook for the National Licensee's Certificate On-Licence*, published by the BII, January 2000. Appendix A explains the procedure and etiquette in force in the Licensing Court.

6. For example, the Section 68 Supper Hour Certificate, the Section 77 Special Hours Certificate, the Section 70 Extended Hours Order, the General Order of Exemption, the Special Order of Exemption, the Occasional Licence and the Public Entertainment Licence (Music, Singing and Dancing or MSD) are all provisions under the licensing laws for various types of alcohol sale.

7. Published by the Justices' Clerks' Society.

8. See also *Handbook for the National Licensee's Certificate On-Licence*, BII, 2000.

9. These are available from the Performing Rights Society and from Phonographic Performance Limited. For showing videos or DVDs you need a Video Performance Limited Licence. See Appendix 5.

Freehold, leasehold or franchise?

Tenure: freehold

The freehold of a property is the outright ownership of it. This means that it is yours to sell, let, alter or demolish (subject to planning and other regulations). Owning the freehold is a relatively good way to predict the costs of occupation (leasehold rents can vary dramatically). If you plan to expand, remember that owning adjoining properties will give you some scope to expand or alter usage.

Buying the freehold makes sense if you plan to be in this location long term or if you plan to expand. In the latter case, two adjacent freehold buildings owned by the same business would generally have a combined value that is greater than the sum of their individual values.

Although buying the freehold is the most expensive option, it allows you more freedom and control, releases you from rent reviews and, in times of rising property values, means that you have assets that appreciate independently of the business – and enhance your capacity to borrow more money, should you wish to.

A freehold can also give you greater scope – in accordance with all the appropriate laws and planning regulations – to alter the business, extend the building and change things as the market changes. Provided it is in keeping with local planning laws, you can change the use and offerings of the business, spruce it up to sell, use it to finance more purchases and so on.

Tenure: leasehold

Modern leases exist for all manner of businesses, and are of particular importance where a property-based business is concerned, particularly in the hospitality and retail sectors. They are often the only way of running a property in city centres, where opportunities to buy freeholds are scarce. Leases are long and complicated documents, and it is wise to read them alongside your professional advisor (lawyer or valuer) and to prepare a summary of the main points of the lease – duration, rent, rights, liabilities and so on. From this you can draw up a worst and best case plan.

A lease essentially gives you the use of the property for an agreed term, for which you pay a rent. The greatest advantage of the lease is that you do not have to find the capital to buy the building you do business from. With an investment in a leasehold business you are usually investing predominantly in the business rather than in bricks and mortar. It may be that taking a lease allows you to use a larger or better-placed property than you might otherwise be able to afford. This, in turn, might increase your turnover and improve your cash flow, particularly in the crucial early stages.

All leases can be a risk, since you are liable to pay the rent whether your business floats or sinks. The more established the business, the less risk there is. The newer the business, the greater the risk. Most modern leases tend to be between 10 and 35 years with rent reviews every 5 years. Longer leases of, say, 50 years or more are normally ground leases; these tend to carry only a nominal rent, sometimes referred to as a peppercorn rent, and in such cases the business can usually be valued almost as if freehold.

Longer leases tend to be more saleable and it is easier for you (or someone buying from you) to raise money to buy a relatively long lease. Once you take a lease you may be able to sell your leasehold interest to another tenant. This is called *assignment* or *assigning the lease* and can be quite a complex process. Some leases contain a prohibition on assignment and most others contain a requirement to obtain the landlord's prior written consent to an assignment. However, you should be aware that you may still be responsible to the landlord if the new tenant fails to meet the terms of the lease.[1] (See page 217.)

Always try to see the original lease, which may be on deposit at a bank or solicitors. Pay particular attention to your obligations under the lease. These are called *covenants*. A covenant might influence further development, restrict use, or affect the operation of your business (type and hours of trade) in some way you may not be able to anticipate. Attached to the lease will be details of the rent reviews, deeds of variation, and authorised alterations.

The most important covenant is, in fact, the requirement to pay rent on due dates. Make sure that you know when the rent is due to be paid and whether it is subject to VAT. Other covenants might cover your obligations to repair and maintain the building, to pay rates, to meet a range of statutory requirements (planning, public health, licensing), and to leave the property in good order at the end of the lease. The landlord will often be required to insure the property, although they may be able to reclaim insurance costs from you.

Under the lease a landlord may be able to prepare at various times – often at the end of a lease – what is called a *Schedule of Dilapidations* (sometimes known as a *Schedule of Condition*). These are repairs which are necessary and which could be expensive. If you take on a lease, you may find that the landlord can immediately serve a Schedule of Dilapidations. If you are purchasing a lease, you should check in your negotiations with the current tenant that the cost of any repairs has been reflected in the premium (price) to be paid. A thorough survey should give you the information you need to negotiate from a position of strength.

Under the Landlord and Tenant Act 1954 some

tenants of commercial property have a statutory right to renew their lease at the end of the original term. The process is regulated by Part II of the Act and requires the serving of various notices and counter-notices by landlord and tenant. The protection does not apply to those who occupy a property under a licence agreement or a tenancy at will.

A tenant's right to renew may, however, be defeated if the landlord successfully shows any of the following:

- Persistent delay in paying rent.
- The tenant has not maintained the property in accordance with the obligations under the lease.
- The tenant has not kept to the other obligations within the lease, or the occupation of the property has included breaches of law (eg planning regulations).
- The landlord wishes to redevelop the property.
- The landlord has offered the tenant suitable alternative accommodation.
- The landlord wishes to occupy the property (certain restrictions apply to this).
- The tenant has a sub-lease of only part of the property and the landlord can make more money by letting the property as a whole.

The courts can renew a lease for a maximum of 14 years. If the landlord successfully opposes the tenant's application for renewal of the lease where the tenant is not at fault, then the tenant is entitled to compensation under a formula incorporated within the Act.

A landlord can avoid a tenant gaining rights to renew the lease under the 1954 Act if, prior to the lease being granted, the landlord and the tenant obtain what is known as a 'contracting out' order from a court. Often a landlord will insist on such a court order being granted as a pre-condition of granting the tenant a lease so that the landlord can be sure of getting the property back at the end of the lease.

Leases of public houses often contain a "tie" (see Chapter 5, page 93) which requires the tenant to buy some or all of the products sold in the pub from the landlord, or from nominated suppliers. Ties vary in nature from lease to lease and should be taken into account when formulating your Business Plan. A tie may require you to stock certain products and may contain a provision for a "guest ale", allowing you freedom to stock one cask-conditioned beer of your choice. Some public houses are let on tenancy agreements which are generally short (one to five years) and non-assignable.

Before you enter into a lease, there is a long checklist of matters you should look out for. These include the following:

- The term of the lease. Is it right for you?
- Have you done a full Structural Survey?
- Have you checked the frequency of rent reviews? Many leases have "upward-only" rent reviews.
- What are the procedures for settling disputes (including rent reviews) if you are unable to reach a negotiated settlement?
- Do you have the right to assign (or sub-let) the property? Does this require the landlord's permission?
- Are you aware of any restrictions in the lease that could harm your business?
- Can you alter the property?
- Does the lease contain a break clause, whether landlord's, tenant's or mutual? A landlord's break is for situations where, for example, the property may be required for redevelopment. A tenant's break is to enable the tenant to terminate the lease and bring their obligations to an end. This could be useful following a rent review where the rent has risen to an unacceptable level. Some breaks can be mutual, with both landlord and tenant having the right to exercise the break. However, a landlord's break or a

mutual break is not suitable for a tenant hoping to build up goodwill (eg in a pub or restaurant) as this would depress the value of the business.

Franchise

Some newcomers to the world of business prefer to go down the route of franchising, which allows them the satisfaction of owning their own business, but without the worry of trying to establish their own style of operation or brand. The décor, lists of products and services you can offer, staff uniforms and training, company culture and even the marketing all come from head office. You will have ready access to finance and advice. You will make regular payments to the franchisor, often related to turnover; these should cover training, equipment, advertising and other particulars set out in the franchise agreement between you and the franchisor. However, the trade-off is that you have little scope for imagination and self-expression in such a business. The British Franchise Association says the more popular use of the term "franchising" has arisen from the development of what is called "business format franchising". This it defines as "the granting of a licence by one person (the franchisor) to another (the franchisee), which entitles the franchisee to trade under the trade mark/trade name of the franchisor and to make use of an entire package, comprising all the elements necessary to establish a previously untrained person in the business and to run it with continual assistance on a predetermined basis".

Before you sign a franchise agreement, you must be clear about the following:

- What are the fees you must pay to the franchisor?
- What is the franchisor's history? Talk to other franchisees to find out about this.
- What are the start-up costs? Typically, these will include an initial fee, on-going management service

fees – usually based on a percentage of annual turnover or mark-ups on supplies – advertising costs, and tie-in agreements to buy equipment or goods from the franchisor.

- The terms of the franchise agreement and its territorial extent.
- The intellectual property rights involved.
- The selling-on of the franchise to a new franchisee.

For more information about franchising, contact the British Franchise Association or log on to its web site: www.british-franchise.org.uk

Note

1. Under the Privity of Contract Rule (relating to leases granted before 1 January 1996), the original lessee was made responsible to the landlord, whoever subsequently took on the lease. The Landlord and Tenant (Covenants) Act 1995, which abolished the Privity Rule for new leases, gave landlords the right to ask for guarantees from the original lessee.

Structural Survey and Valuation Report

There are broadly six types of building survey:

- Survey carried out for a prospective purchaser before they make an offer to buy. This is a Structural Survey.
- Survey carried out by an insurer before insuring a property.
- Survey carried out by an owner before altering a property.
- Survey commissioned during a dispute between a landlord and tenant over repairs.
- Survey commissioned in order to value and then market a property.
- Survey commissioned as part of a business valuation.

These kinds of survey may, of course, overlap in practice. One building may have had many surveys, and they make up its essential history. It is certainly useful to see any past surveys – if you can – before you commission your own, either as a stand-alone building survey or as part of a business valuation.

Property has a life of its own whether or not a business is being run from it. A private house can be converted into a nursing home, a pub can be converted into a private house, a shop can become a workshop (assuming, in each case, the necessary planning consent can be obtained). The building is one of the prime assets of the business. As an asset, it can appreciate or depreciate over time depending on trends in the property market (which, in turn, depend on a variety of economic and fiscal circumstances), on how it is maintained, and on how changes in the neighbourhood affect the building and its use. The value of any business that owns or leases property is therefore closely related to the value of property as a whole.

Structural Survey

A survey of the business buildings is therefore an essential part of buying the business. A good Structural Survey will address the three fixed points of every property-based business – location, tenure and buildings – but it will focus primarily on the buildings. Such a survey should be carried out by a structural surveyor. Surveying properties is a specialised professional matter and it is not something possible for the layman to do. It is therefore relatively expensive.

A good Structural Survey will consider many issues:

1. The site of the building, its boundaries, its extent and any environmental concerns about the site.[1] (See page 224.)
2. Access. There should be a thorough look at access to the premises, car parking, disabled access, shared access and so on.
3. The description and condition of the building, its state, its inherent defects. Examples are the state of repair of its roof, walls, windows, foundations, floors; whether or not it has woodworm, dry rot, wet rot; whether it needs insulation, double glazing, and so on. It should also give an idea of the decorative condition of the building, although this may vary from room to room. Establishing the structural state and decorative condition of a building is a first step in establishing if there are any obliga-

tions to maintain and repair the building as part of a lease. Photos and videos are useful in this regard.

4. Repairs. A survey should reveal where repairs are necessary and when, although the cost of repairs will depend on the builder doing them. This is of particular value if you plan to sign a lease that commits you to repair, redecorate and maintain the property.

5. The appropriateness of the building for the purpose you plan for it. This is a complex area requiring a detailed knowledge of local and national building regulations as they apply to specific uses. It will include aspects of health and safety law, security, floor loadings, energy supplies, fire prevention and the use of public space.[2] This can only be done by a qualified surveyor.

6. The accommodation. The number of rooms, their size and use. Rooms with special use – the kitchen, bar, dispensary, bathrooms for the disabled – should be carefully surveyed and described. There may be specific comments about the condition of the paintwork, wallpaper, windows and flooring.

7. Whether the rooms or communal space comply with current legislation – for example, with the Required Minimum Standards in care homes – and with health and safety regulations with regard to fire exits.

8. Services. The utilities (electricity, water and drainage, gas, central heating, kitchen facilities) and their condition. All properties from time to time may need to be rewired and replumbed.

If the property is leasehold, your structural surveyor should provide a Schedule of Dilapidations or Condition (see Appendix 2, page 213). This is really a snapshot of the condition of a building and is useful to limit your liability for repairs if the property is in poor condition. Such a report is essential if you are considering taking a new lease and you are negotiating with the landlord. If there is an existing lease, and you are not negotiating direct with the landlord, a Schedule of Condition can be of use in negotiating the price you pay for the business.

Valuation Report

While a Structural Survey covers the building, a Valuation Report covers the value of the business. This will, of course, include the value of its assets – the buildings – and will therefore be related to the Structural Survey. There is no direct relationship between the building reinstatement costs (a figure often given in a Structural Survey for fire insurance purposes) and the market value of the same property. A valuation is an extremely useful process and is part of the assessment and management of risk. Before you buy a shop, pub, hotel, restaurant, children's day nursery or care home, it is prudent to have a thorough survey and valuation. Without them, many lenders will not lend; and without them, you may not know the value of the business (as distinct from the seller's asking price) or the liabilities you may take on if you have not researched adequately.

A Valuation Report allows you to look both back into the accounts and forward towards any liabilities or difficulties you may be taking on. A valuation will cover some matters (local search, title) which your solicitor will research in detail, and it is often valuable to have a double check on the information before you make the important and irrevocable decision to buy. The more information you have about all aspects of the business, the better. A valuation should be done by someone who is familiar with the particular type of business that you are hoping to buy into.

A good Valuation Report will give you the market value of the business. It assesses accounts, goodwill, trading prospects, probable markets, location, competition and planning. There is no definitive formula or form for a Valuation Report, but it is important that the report is thorough and clear in style. If done well, a Valuation Report will produce facts about the business which you can call on when you start to negotiate your price with the seller. The valuer – often someone acting for a bank or mortgage loan company – will produce what they call reconstituted accounts. These are accounts which have had removed from them all those factors which are peculiar and particular to the present owner. You can then see exactly how profitable the business is without calculating any of your own expenses. A valuation will give you credibility should you need to borrow money; and it may help you avoid buying a business which is not right for you.

The Valuation Report should state whether the property is freehold or leasehold and, in the latter case, set out the principal terms of the lease. It should tell you the length of the lease, whether the lease is renewable or assignable, whether it has protection under the 1954 Landlord and Tenant Act, when rent reviews are due, and what your rights and responsibilities are. Leases vary between commercial sectors; a lease on a pub is unlikely to be the same as a lease on a children's day nursery or a convenience store. It is hard to generalise about leases simply because most business properties, if leasehold, have only one lease and that lease is unique. Freeholds are more straightforward, giving you ownership of the property in perpetuity.

The Valuation Report should include a check with the local planning office that there is no problem with the current business use, or with its continuation. You should know if the building is subject to any kind of preservation order, if it is listed, if there are any rights of way across the property, if there are planning restrictions on either development or particular trades in the area – if all goes wrong, you may want to change the use of the building. At the same time your solicitor should check with the local planning officers for any intended construction of any kind in the area which might affect you: new roads, new industrial sites, new retail parks and so on. Read the local newspapers to get a sense of how much planning and building is taking place.

Every domestic property in the UK attracts a community charge, and most commercial properties attract commercial rates set by the Inland Revenue. The rateable value of a business property is, roughly speaking, its market rental value; this in turn is multiplied by a figure called the uniform business rate (UBR) which is adjusted annually. The tax is due on the building and must be paid by the occupier. There is a system of revaluations, appeals, transitional relief and empty occupation rates, all of which may alter the Inland Revenue's assessment.

Most business properties have fixtures and fittings – such as furniture, plant and machinery/equipment. The vendor should indicate what is included in the sale price. Furniture, carpets, curtains, kitchen equipment, lighting, displays or any fittings specific to the business should all be noted and accounted for; in any business, the vendor should declare exactly what is included in the sale, what items are leased or rented and spell out if they are planning to remove anything which is currently part of the business as opposed to the family home.

Any stock being sold with the business should be the subject of a separate valuation by professional stocktakers, and should take account of perishable and non-perishable items, and the cost of replacing or replenishing them. This is a specialist matter, requiring expert advice, and is usually carried out on either the day, or just before, you take over the business.

The final item of value within an established business is its goodwill. The business valuation should give you a clear sense of how much the seller is asking for this. The goodwill of a business assumes that the purchaser will be reasonably competent and will continue to trade in a similar way with much the same clients as before. If, for example, a business goes upmarket or downmarket its goodwill is essentially lost because it is reaching out to new clients and not capitalising on the goodwill of existing ones. Goodwill can be the value of a famous brand, an established reputation of a renowned chef, restaurateur or hotelier, or some other intangible benefit. Here it can be summed up as an assessment of the worth of the reputation of the business and its ability to make profits.

Notes

1. These environmental concerns are covered in the Environment Protection Act 1990 and the Environment Act 1995.
2. The Building Act 1984 and consequent Building Regulations are the most important here.

APPENDIX 4

The legal foundation of your business

There are four ways in which you can trade: as Sole Trader, Partnership, Limited Liability Partnership and Limited Company.

Sole Trader

The simplest form of business is as a *Sole Trader*, either in your own name or a business name. As a Sole Trader you own your business and keep all the profits you make after tax but, equally, any business losses are your losses. Your business is indistinguishable from you personally.

Partnership

You may want to trade as a *Partnership*. This is an association of at least two people. It is advisable to instruct your solicitors to draw up a *Deed of Partnership* to clarify such matters as division of profits and losses, partners' responsibilities, drawings, expenses and dispute resolution. Partners have unlimited liability for the total debts of the business partnership, both jointly and severally. However, while the partnership deed may say that losses are to be split equally, you should note that if your partner(s) can't or won't pay, you will be personally liable for all the losses. If no Deed of Partnership is drawn up, the partnership will be governed by the Partnership Act, which provides that all profits and losses are shared equally.

Limited Liability Partnership

An alternative to a partnership is the *Limited Liability Partnership* (LLP). While this was originally developed for large accounting and law firms, any business can form itself as an LLP. The principle is that LLPs are separate bodies and that they have members rather than partners or shareholders; they are, like companies, a legal entity distinct from their members. There is also a requirement to have at least two "designated members" who have responsibilities comparable to those of company directors. It should be noted that "members" is not a term unique to LLPs as shareholders in companies are also known as members. An LLP removes the joint and several liability of partnerships; this is replaced with liability limited to the total assets of the partnership. LLP status is an alternative to full incorporation, particularly for care homes where there may be tax advantages when it comes to the selling of individual homes or the whole business. The LLP is essentially a halfway stage, between traditional partnerships and companies. However, the trade off in setting up an LLP is that liability is limited, but a partnership business has to be made public in that there is a duty to file accounts and returns at Companies House. To set up an LLP you need to file form LLP2 at Companies House and pay a registration fee. A partnership deed is still likely to be required and you are likely to require the advice of a solicitor in these matters.

Limited Company

By forming a *Limited Company*, you will reduce your personal liability but you will have additional responsibilities and greater public accountability as a result of the provisions of the Companies Act as you are also likely to be a director. A Limited Company is a separate legal entity. Normally, there would be no liability on the part of directors, unless they are shareholders; however, it may be necessary to give personal guarantees in order to gain finance. For example, where a company is new and has no trading history and little in the way of assets, in order to secure their loans, banks will expect a charge over the property of the directors (ie a mortgage) so they have some chance of recovering their money if the company fails. Also, directors' personal assets are available in limited circumstances to pay creditors. These include an insolvent liquidation, where the directors may be held responsible for the debts of the company if it can be shown that they continued to trade at a time when they knew or ought to have known that there was no reasonable prospect of the company avoiding insolvency.

If you decide to form a Limited Company rather than trading as a Partnership or Sole Trader, there are certain formalities that need to be complied with. Having first checked that the name you wish to use is available, you will need to file form G10 (which sets out the address of the registered office and the particulars of the persons who are to be the first directors and secretary) and also form G12 (which is a statutory declaration of compliance with the requirements of the Companies Act), together with a copy of the Memorandum of Association and the Articles of Association. The Memorandum of Association is the document governing the company's relationship with third parties and sets out the purpose for which the company is formed, the amount of its share capital and name. The Memorandum of Association should be signed by two subscribers and their signatures must be witnessed. The Articles of Association govern the company's internal relationship with its shareholders. Commonly, a private company limited by shares will adopt Table A, which is a standard set of regulations with some amendments. Assuming the Registrar of Companies is satisfied that the incorporation documents are in order, a Certificate of Incorporation will be issued, which is conclusive evidence that the requirements of the Companies Act have been met. You can either form the company yourself, instruct a solicitor to complete the forms for you or purchase an off-the-shelf company from formation agents. A shelf company is one that has already been formed but has never traded. The formation agent sells you the company with standard Memorandum and Articles, and transfers the share(s) to your nominee(s). The existing director and secretary will resign so you can appoint your own. As the documentation is not drawn-up specifically for your business its standard format may be inappropriate for your needs. It is advisable that you seek the advice of a solicitor on this issue.

APPENDIX 5

Resources

Accounting Standards Board
7th Floor, Holborn Hall, 100 Gray's Inn Road,
London WC1X 8AL
Tel: 020 7404 8818
Web site: www.asb.org.uk
E-mail: tech.enquiries@asb.org.uk

Alliance of Independent Retailers
Bank Chambers, 5-9 St Nicholas Street,
Worcester WR1 1UW
Tel: 01905 612733
Web site: www.indretailer.co.uk
E-mail: alliance@indretailer.co.uk

Association of Convenience Stores
Federation House, 17 Farnborough Street,
Farnborough, Hampshire GU14 8AG
Tel: 01252 515001
Web site: www.cstoreretailing.co.uk
E-mail: acs@acs.org.uk

British Association for Early Childhood Education
136 Cavell Street, London E1 2JA
Tel: 020 7539 5400
Web site: www.early-education.org.uk
E-mail: office@early-education.org.uk

British Beer and Pub Association (formerly The Brewers & Licensed Retailers Association)
Market Towers, 1 Nine Elms Lane, London SW8 5NQ
Tel: 020 7627 9191
Web site: www.beerandpub.com
E-mail: enquiries@beerandpub.com

British Chambers of Commerce
Manning House, 22 Carlisle Place, London SW1P 1JA
Tel: 020 7565 2000
Web site: www.britishchambers.org.uk
E-mail: info@britishchambers.org.uk

British Franchise Association
Thames View, Newtown Road,
Henley-on-Thames,
Oxfordshire RG9 1HG
Tel: 01491 578050
Web site: www.british-franchise.org.uk
E-mail: mailroom@british-franchise.org.uk

British Hospitality Association
Queens House, 55-56 Lincoln's Inn Fields,
London WC2A 3BH
Tel: 020 7404 7744
Web site: www.bha-online.org.uk
E-mail: bha@bha.org.uk

British Institute of Innkeeping
Wessex House, 80 Park Street, Camberley,
Surrey GU15 3PT
Tel: 01276 684449
Web site: www.bii.org
E-mail: reception@bii.org

British Retail Consortium
5 Grafton Street, London W1X 3LB
Tel: 020 76471500
Web site: www.brc.org.uk
E-mail: reception@brc.org.uk

British Tourist Authority
Trade Help Desk,
Thames Tower, Black's Road,
London W6 9EL
Tel: 020 8563 3186
Web sites: www.bta.org.uk and
www.tourismtrade.org.uk
E-mail: tradehelpdesk@bta.org.uk

British Venture Capital Association
Essex House, 12-13 Essex Street, London WC2R 3AA
Tel: 020 7240 3846
Web site: www.bvca.co.uk
E-mail: bvca@bvca.co.uk

Business Connect Wales
Regional offices covering North Wales, Mid Wales,
West Wales and South East Wales.
Tel: 08457 969798
Web site: www.businessconnect.org.uk
E-mail: executive@businessconnect.org.uk

Cabinet Office - Performance and Innovation Unit
4th Floor, Admiralty Arch, The Mall,
London SW1A 2WH
Tel: 020 7276 1447
Web site: www.cabinet-office.gov.uk/innovation
E-mail: piu@cabinet-office.x.gsi.gov.uk

Caring Times **(trade journal)**
Hawker Publications,
2nd Floor, Culvert House, Culvert Road,
London SW11 5DH
Tel: 020 7720 2108
Web site: www.careinfo.org
E-mail: hawker@hawkerpubs.demon.co.uk

Caring UK **(trade journal)**
47 Church Street, Barnsley,
South Yorkshire S70 2AS
Tel: 01226 734634
Web site: None.
E-mail: caringuk@yorkshire-web.co.uk

Caterer & Hotelkeeper **(trade journal)**
Quadrant House,
The Quadrant, Sutton,
Surrey SM2 5AS
Tel: 020 8652 3221
Web site: www.caterer.com
E-mail: No general enquiries e-mail address available.

Chartered Institute of Marketing
Moor Hall, Cookham,
Maidenhead,
Berkshire SL6 9QH
Tel: 01628 427500
Web site: www.cim.co.uk
E-mail: marketing@cim.co.uk

Child Accident Prevention Trust
4th Floor, 18-20 Farringdon Lane,
London EC1R 3HA
Tel: 020 7608 3828
Web site: www.capt.org.uk
E-mail: safe@capt.org.uk

Christie & Co
Please see the contact details on pages 246–248.

Christie First
4 & 6 York Street, London W1H 1FA
Tel: 020 7535 5000
Web site: www.christiefirst.com
E-mail: enquiries@christiefirst.com

Companies House
Crown Way, Cardiff, CF14 3UZ
Tel: 0870 3333636
Web site: www.companieshouse.gov.uk
E-mail: enquiries@companieshouse.gov.uk

Community Care (trade journal)
Quadrant House, The Quadrant, Sutton, SM2 5AS
Tel: 020 8652 4861
Web site: www.community-care.co.uk
E-mail: comcare@community-care.co.uk

Convenience Store (trade journal)
William Reed Publishing,
Broadfield Park, Crawley, West Sussex RH11 9RT
Tel: 01293 610400
Web site: www.william-reed.co.uk/magazines
E-mail: No general enquiries e-mail address available.

Croner CCH Group

145 London Road, Kingston Upon Thames,
Surrey KT2 6SR
Tel: 020 8547 3333
Web site: www.croner.cch.co.uk
E-mail: info@croner.cch.co.uk

Daltons Weekly (trade journal)

C.I. Tower, St George's Square, New Malden,
Surrey KT3 4JA
Tel: 020 8949 6199
Web site: www.daltons.co.uk
E-mail: daltons@daltons.co.uk

Day Care Trust

21 St George's Road, London SE1 6ES
Tel: 020 7840 3350
Web site: www.daycaretrust.org.uk
E-mail: info@daycaretrust.org.uk

Department for Education and Skills

Public Enquiry Unit
Sanctuary Buildings, Great Smith Street,
London SW1P 3BT
Tel: 0870 000 2288
Web site: www.dfes.gov.uk
E-mail: info@dfes.gsi.gov.uk

Department of Health

Richmond House,
79 Whitehall,
London SW1A 2NS
Tel: 020 7210 4850
Web site: www.doh.gov.uk
E-mail: dhmail@doh.gsi.gov.uk

Department of Trade and Industry

1 Victoria Street,
London SW1H 0ET
Tel: 020 7215 5000
Web site: www.dti.gov.uk
E-mail: dti.enquiries@dti.gsi.gov.uk

Dine Out (trade journal)
Africa House, 64-78 Kingsway, London WC2B 6AH
Tel: 020 7831 8727
Web site: www.ragb.co.uk
E-mail: No general enquiries e-mail address available.

Employers' Helpline (DTI)
DTI Enquiry Unit, 1 Victoria Street, London SW1H 0ET
Tel: 0345 143143 / 020 7215 5000
Web site: www.dti.gov.uk
E-mail: dti.enquiries@dti.gsi.gov.uk

English Tourism Council (English Tourist Board)
Thames Tower, Blacks Road, London W6 9EL
Tel: 020 8563 3000
Web Site: www.englishtourism.org.uk
E-mail: help@englishtourism.org

Federation of Small Businesses
2 Catherine Place, Westminster, London SW1E 6HF
Tel: 020 7592 8100
Web site: www.fsb.org.uk
E-mail: london@fsb.org.uk

Fitzhugh Publications
12 Riverview Grove, London W4 3QJ
Tel: 020 8995 1752
Web site: None.
E-mail: No general enquiries e-mail address available.

Foodservice Intelligence
84 Uxbridge Road, London W13 8RA
Tel: 020 8799 3202
Web site: www.fsintelligence.com
E-mail: No general enquiries e-mail address available.

Grocer (trade journal)
William Reed Publishing, Broadfield Park, Crawley,
West Sussex RH11 9RT
Tel: 01293 610400
Web site: www.william-reed.co.uk/magazines
E-mail: No general enquiries e-mail address available.

Home Office

Customer Information Service,
7th Floor, 50 Queen Anne's Gate,
London SW1H 9AT
Tel: 0870 000 1585
Web site: www.homeoffice.gov.uk
E-mail: public.enquiries@homeoffice.gsi.gov.uk

Hospitality (trade journal)

191 Trinity Road, London SW17 7HN
Tel: 020 8772 7400
Web site: www.hcima.org.uk
E-mail: general@hcima.org.uk

Hospitality Training Foundation

3rd Floor, International House, High Street, Ealing,
London W5 5DB
Tel: 020 8579 2400
Web sites: www.htf.org.uk and www.openallhours.org
E-mail: nto@htf.org.uk

Hotel & Catering International Management Association

191 Trinity Road, London SW17 7HN
Tel: 020 8772 7400
Web site: www.hcima.org.uk
E-mail: admin@hcima.co.uk

Independent Healthcare Association

Westminster Tower, 3 Albert Embankment,
London SE1 7SP
Tel: 020 7793 4620
Web site: www.iha.org.uk
E-mail: info@iha.org.uk

Independent Retail News (trade journal)

Cumulus Business Media,
Anne Boleyn House, 9-13 Ewell Road, Sutton,
Surrey SM3 8BZ
Tel: 020 8643 6207
Web site: www.irn-talkingshop.co.uk
E-mail: everyone@cumulusmedia.co.uk

Institute of Directors
116-123 Pall Mall, London SW1Y 5ED
Tel: 020 7766 8866
Web Site: www.iod.co.uk
E-mail: enquiries@iod.com

Justices' Clerks' Society
2nd Floor, Port of Liverpool Building, Pier Head,
Liverpool L3 1BY
Tel: 0151 255 0790
Web site: www.jc-society.co.uk
E-mail: honsec@jc-society.co.uk

Kids' Clubs Network
Bellerive House, 3 Muirfield Crescent, London E14 9SZ
Tel: 020 7512 2100
Web site: www.kidsclubs.org.uk
E-mail: information.office@kidsclubs.co.uk

King's Fund
11-13 Cavendish Square, London W1G 0AN
Tel: 020 7307 2400
Web site: www.kingsfund.org.uk
E-mail: library@kingsfund.org.uk

Laing & Buisson
29 Angel Gate, City Road, London EC1V 2PT
Tel: 020 7923 5398
Web site: www.laingbuisson.co.uk
E-mail: info@laingbuisson.co.uk

The Learning + Skills Council (formerly The Training and Enterprise Council)
101 Lockhurst Lane, Foleshill, Coventry CV6 5SF
Tel: 024 7658 2761
Web site: www.lsc.gov.uk
E-mail: info@lsc.gov.uk

Licensed Victuallers' Association
The association is organised regionally and there is no
national contact point. Its name may also differ from
region to region (eg National Federation of Licensed

Victuallers). Find your local contact details through either directory enquiries or your local telephone directory.

Local Enterprise Companies (covering Scotland by geographical area)

Scottish Enterprise, 5 Atlantic Quay, 150 Broomielaw, Glasgow G2 8LU
Tel: 0845 607 8787 or 0141 228 2000 (general enquiries)
Web site: www.scottish-enterprise.com
E-mail: network.helpline@scotent.co.uk

Mintel International

18-19 Long Lane, London EC1A 9PL
Tel: 020 7606 4533
Web site: www.mintel.com
E-mail: enquiries@mintel.com

Morning Advertiser (trade journal)

William Reed Publishing, Broadfield Park, Crawley, West Sussex RH11 9RT
Tel: 01293 610400
Web site: www.william-reed.co.uk/magazines
E-mail: No general enquiries e-mail address available.

National Association of Self Employed

Lynch House, 91 Mansfield Road, Nottingham NG1 3FN
Tel: 0115 947 5046
Web site: Under construction at the time of writing.
E-mail: nasgbni@btclick.com

National Audit Office

The Information Centre Helpdesk, 157-197 Buckingham Palace Road, London SW1W 9SP
Tel: 020 7798 7264
Web site: www.nao.gsi.gov.uk
E-mail: enquiries@nao.gsi.gov.uk

National Care Homes Association

4th Floor, 45/49 Leather Lane, London EC1N 7TJ
Tel: 020 7831 7090
Web site: www.ncha.gb.com
E-mail: ncha@btclick.com

National Care Standards Commission
St Nicholas' Buildings, St Nicholas Street,
Newcastle upon Tyne NE1 1NB
Tel: 0191 233 3500
Web site: www.doh.gov.uk/ncsc
E-mail: None at the time of writing.

National Childminding Association
8 Masons Hill, Bromley, Kent BR2 9EY
Tel: 020 8461 6100
Web site: www.ncma.org.uk
E-mail: info@ncma.org.uk

National Day Nursery Association
16 New North Parade, Huddersfield,
West Yorkshire HD1 5JP
Tel: 0870 7700449
Web site: ndna.org.uk
E-mail: info@ndna.org.uk

National Federation of Enterprise Agencies
Trinity Gardens, 9-11 Bromham Road,
Bedford MK40 2UQ
Tel: 01234 354055
Web sites: www.nfea.com and
www.smallbusinessadvice.org.uk
E-mail: No general enquiries e-mail address available.

National Federation of Retail Newsagents
Yeoman House, Sekforde Street,
London EC1R 0HF
Tel: 020 7253 4225
Web site: www.nfrn.org.uk
E-mail: info@nfrn.org.uk

National Federation of SubPostmasters
Evelyn House,
22 Windlesham Gardens,
Shoreham by Sea, West Sussex BN43 5AZ
Tel: 01273 452324
Web site: www.subpostmasters.org.uk
E-mail: nfsp@subpostmasters.org.uk

National Restaurant Association (USA)
1200 17th Street, NW,
Washington DC 20036
Tel: +1 202 3315900 / 8004245156
Web site: www.restaurant.org
E-mail: info@dineout.org

Northern Ireland Hotels Federation
Midland Building,
Whitla Street, Belfast BT15 1JP
Tel: 028 9035 1110
Web site: www.nihf.co.uk
E-mail: nihf@bigfoot.com

***Nursery Management Today* (trade journal)**
Hawker Publications,
2nd Floor, Culvert House,
Culvert Road, London SW11 5DH
Tel: 020 7720 2108
Web site: www.careinfo.org
E-mail: hawker@hawkerpubs.demon.co.uk

***Nursery World* (trade journal)**
Admiral House, 66-68 East Smithfield,
London E1W 1BX
Tel: 020 7782 3000
Web site: www.nursery-world.com
E-mail: No general enquiries e-mail address available.

***Off Licence News* (trade journal)**
William Reed Publishing,
Broadfield Park, Crawley,
West Sussex RH11 9RT
Tel: 01293 610400
Web site: www.william-reed.co.uk
E-mail: No general enquiries e-mail address available.

Office for National Statistics
1 Drummond Gate, London SW1V 2QQ
Tel: 020 7233 9233
Web site: www.statistics.gov.uk
E-mail: info@statistics.gov.uk

Office of Fair Trading
Fleetbank House, 2-6 Salisbury Square, London EC4Y 8JX
Tel: 08457 224499
Web site: www.oft.gov.uk
E-mail: enquiries@oft.gov.uk

Office for Standards in Education (OFSTED)
Alexandra House, 33 Kingsway, London WC2B 6SE
Tel: 020 7421 6800
Web site: www.ofsted.gov.uk
E-mail: geninfo@ofsted.gov.uk

Performing Rights Society
29-33 Berners Street, London W1T 3AB
Tel: 020 7580 5544
Web site: www.mcps-prs-alliance.co.uk
E-mail: info@mcps-prs-alliance.co.uk

Phonographic Performance Ltd
1 Upper James Street, London W1F 9DE
Tel: 020 7534 1000
Web site: www.ppluk.com
E-mail: No general enquiries e-mail address available.

Post Office Ltd
PO Box 204, Royal Tunbridge Wells, Kent TN4 8BR
Tel: 08457 223344
Web site: www.postoffice.co.uk
E-mail: E-mail access only available through the website.

Post Office Franchise
Post Office Franchise Team, Gavrelle House,
2-14 Bunhill Row, London EC1Y 8HQ
Tel: 020 7847 3534
Web site: None.
E-mail: No general enquiries e-mail address available.

Pre-school Learning Alliance
69 King's Cross Road, London WC1X 9LL
Tel: 020 7833 0991
Web site: www.pre-school.org.uk
E-mail: pla@pre-school.org.uk

Professional Association of Nursery Nurses
2 St James' Court, Friar Gate,
Derby DE1 1BT
Tel: 01332 372337
Web site: www.pat.org.uk
E-mail: pann@pat.org.uk

Publican **(trade journal)**
Quantum House,
19 Scarbrook Road, Croydon,
Surrey CR9 1LX
Tel: 020 8565 4200
Web site: www.thepublican.com
E-mail: No general enquiries e-mail address available.

Qualifications and Curriculum Authority
83 Piccadilly, London W1J 8QA
Tel: 020 7509 5555
Web site: www.qca.org.uk
E-mail: info@qca.org.uk

Quest for Quality
50 Victoria Street, London SW1H 0NW
Tel: 020 7227 0758
Web site: None.
E-mail: enquiries@q4q.co.uk

Registered Nursing Home Association
15 Highfield Road,
Edgbaston,
Birmingham B15 3DU
Tel: 0121 454 2511
Web site: www.rnha.co.uk
E-mail: info@rnha.co.uk

Restaurant Association
Africa House,
64-78 Kingsway,
London WC2B 6AH
Tel: 020 7831 8727
Web site: www.ragb.co.uk
E-mail: info@ragb.co.uk

Restaurant Business (trade journal)
Dewberry Boyes, Apex House,
London Road
Northfleet, Gravesend DA11 9JA
Tel: 01474 574436
Web site: None.
E-mail: rest.edit@wilmington.co.uk

Retail Newsagent (trade journal)
11 Angel Gate, City Road,
London EC1V 2SD
Tel: 020 7689 0600
Web site: www.worldofmagazines.co.uk
E-mail: rn@newtrade.co.uk

Retail Week (trade journal)
Angel House, 338-346 Goswell Road,
London EC1V 7QP
Tel: 020 7520 1775
Web site: www.4retail.net
E-mail: No general enquiries e-mail address available.

Royal Institution of Chartered Surveyors
12 Great George Street, Parliament Square,
London SW1P 3AD
Tel: 020 7222 7000
Web site: www.rics.org
E-mail: contactrics@rics.org.uk

Royal Institution of Chartered Surveyors in Scotland
9 Manor Place,
Edinburgh EH3 7DN
Tel: 0131 225 7078
Web site: www.rics-scotland.org.uk
E-mail: No general enquiries e-mail address available.

Scottish Care
Weston House, 123 Moss Street,
Keith AB55 5EZ
Tel: 01542 887791
Web site: www.scottishcare.org.uk
E-mail: No general enquiries e-mail address available.

Scottish Caterer (trade journal)
Peebles Media Group,
Bergius House, Clifton Street,
Glasgow G3 7LA
Tel: 0141 567 6000
Web site: www.peeblesmedia.com
E-mail: info@peeblesmedia.com

Scottish Grocer (trade journal)
Peebles Media Group,
Bergius House, Clifton Street,
Glasgow G3 7LA
Tel: 0141 567 6000
Web site: www.peeblesmedia.com
E-mail: info@peeblesmedia.com

Scottish Licensed Trade Association
10 Walker Street, Edinburgh EH3 7LA
Tel: 0131 225 5169
Web site: Under construction at the time of writing.
E-mail: theslta@aol.com

Scottish Licensed Trade News (trade journal)
Peebles Media Group,
Bergius House, Clifton Street,
Glasgow G3 7LA
Tel: 0141 567 6000
Web site: www.peeblesmedia.com
E-mail: info@peeblesmedia.com

Small Business Gateway
7 West George Street, Glasgow G2 1BQ
Tel: 0845 609 6611
Web site: www.sbgateway.com
E-mail: info@sbgatewayglasgowcity.co.uk

Small Business Service (formerly Business Link)
St Mary's House,
C/o Moorfoot, Sheffield S1 4PQ
Tel: 020 7215 5363 (enquiry line)
Web site: www.businesslink.org.uk
E-mail: No general enquiries e-mail address available.

Society of Licensed Victuallers
London Road, Ascot, Berkshire SL5 8DR
Tel: 01344 884440
Web site: www.slv-online.org.uk
E-mail: info@slv-online.org.uk

Standards Board for England
5th Floor, St Christopher House,
98-104 Southwark Street,
London SE1 0TE
Tel: 020 7921 1800
Web site: www.standardsboard.co.uk
E-mail: enquiries@standardsboard.co.uk

Stationery Office
PO Box 29, Norwich NR3 1GN
Tel: 0870 600 5522
Web site: www.thestationeryoffice.com
E-mail: customer.services@theso.co.uk

SubPostmaster (trade journal)
National Federation of SubPostmasters,
Evelyn House, 22 Windlesham Gardens,
Shoreham by Sea, West Sussex BN43 5ZZ
Tel: 01273 452324
Web site: www.subpostmasters.org.uk
E-mail: nfsp@subpostmasters.org.uk

This Caring Business (trade journal)
Martin Mill, Walker Lane,
Hebden Bridge, West Yorkshire HX7 8SJ
Tel: 01422 847078
Web site: None.
E-mail: vivshep@aol.com

Theme Magazine (trade journal)
Mondiale Publishing,
Waterloo Place, Watson Square,
Stockport SK1 3AZ
Tel: 0161480 3344
Web site: www.mondiale.co.uk
E-mail: theme@mondiale.co.uk

Thomson Directories
296 Farnborough Road,
Farnborough, Surrey GU14 7NU
Tel: 01252 555555
Web site: www.thomson-directories.co.uk
E-mail: bsp@thomweb.co.uk

UK Online for Business
Tel: 0845 715 2000
Web site: ukonlineforbusiness.gov.uk

Video Performance Ltd
1 Upper James Street,
Soho, London W1F 9DE
Tel: 020 7534 1400
Web site: None.
E-mail: None.

Visit Scotland
23 Ravelston Terrace,
Edinburgh EH4 3TP
Tel: 0131 332 2433
Web site: www.visitscotland.com
E-mail: info@stb.gov.uk

Venners
66 George Row, London SE16 4UH
Tel: 020 7500 7500
Web site: www.venners.com
E-mail: enquiries@venners.co.uk

VcsTimeless
249 Upper Third Street,
Witan Gate West,
Milton Keynes MK9 1DS
Tel: 01908 350550
Web site: www.vcstimeless.com
E-mail: enquiries@vcstimeless.com

Christie & Co
office addresses

Christie & Co UK regional offices

Birmingham
Edgbaston House, 3 Duchess Place, Hagley Road,
Birmingham B16 8NH
Tel: 0121 456 1222
Fax: 0121 455 0114
E-mail: birmingham@christie.com

Bristol
Beacon House, Queen's Road, Clifton, Bristol BS8 1QU
Tel: 0117 933 1500
Fax: 0117 933 1501
E-mail: bristol@christie.com

Edinburgh
5 Logie Mill, Beaverbank Office Park, Logie Green Road,
Edinburgh EH7 4HG
Tel: 0131 557 6666
Fax: 0131 557 6000
E-mail: edinburgh@christie.com

Exeter
Kings Wharf, The Quay, Exeter EX2 4AN
Tel: 01392 285600
Fax: 01392 285601
E-mail: exeter@christie.com

Glasgow
120 Bath Street, Glasgow G2 2EN
Tel: 0141 352 7300
Fax: 0141 352 7301
E-mail: glasgow@christie.com

Ipswich
16 Lower Brook Street, Ipswich IP4 1AP
Tel: 01473 256588
Fax: 01473 230071
E-mail: ipswich@christie.com

Leeds
Aquis House, Greek Street, Leeds LS1 5RU
Tel: 0113 389 2700
Fax: 0113 389 2701
E-mail: leeds@christie.com

London
50 Victoria Street, London SW1H 0NW
Tel: 020 7227 0700
Fax: 020 7227 0701
E-mail: enquiries@christie.com

Maidstone
Vaughan Chambers, 4 Tonbridge Road,
Maidstone ME16 8RP
Tel: 01622 656000
Fax: 01622 656001
E-mail: maidstone@christie.com

Manchester
Acresfield, St Ann's Square, Manchester M2 7HA
Tel: 0161 833 3311
Fax: 0161 835 2949
E-mail: manchester@christie.com

Milton Keynes
Chancery House, 199 Silbury Boulevard,
Milton Keynes MK9 1JL
Tel: 01908 206600
Fax: 01908 206606
E-mail: miltonkeynes@christie.com

Newcastle
3 Collingwood Street, Newcastle upon Tyne NE1 1JW
Tel: 0191 222 1740
Fax: 0191 222 1749
E-mail: newcastle@christie.com

Nottingham

Alan House, Clumber Street, Nottingham NG1 3ED
Tel: 0115 948 3100
Fax: 0115 948 3865
E-mail: nottingham@christie.com

Winchester

Star Lane House, Staple Gardens, Winchester SO23 8SR
Tel: 01962 844455
Fax: 01962 840171
E-mail: winchester@christie.com

Christie & Co international offices

London

50 Victoria Street, London SW1H 0NW
Tel: +44 (0) 20 7227 0747
Fax: +44 (0) 20 7227 0750
E-mail: international@christie.com

Paris

39, rue Marbeuf, 75008 Paris, France
Tel: +33 (0) 1 53 96 72 72
Fax +33 (0) 1 53 96 72 82
E-mail: paris@christie.com

Frankfurt

Bockenheimer Landstrasse 93,
60325 Frankfurt am Main, Germany
Tel: + 49 (0) 69 90 74 57-0
Fax + 49 (0) 69 90 74 57-10
E-mail: frankfurt@christie.com

Barcelona

Paseo de Gracia 11, Escalera B, 4º 3ª,
08007 Barcelona, Spain
Tel: +34 93 34 361 61
Fax: +34 93 34 361 60
E-mail: barcelona@christie.com

VISIT OUR WEB SITE
www.christie.com